human rights *first*

Denial and Delay

The Impact of the Immigration Law's "Terrorism Bars" on Asylum Seekers and Refugees in the United States

November 2009

About Human Rights First

Human Rights First believes that building respect for human rights and the rule of law will help ensure the dignity to which every individual is entitled and will stem tyranny, extremism, intolerance, and violence.

Human Rights First protects people at risk: refugees who flee persecution, victims of crimes against humanity or other mass human rights violations, victims of discrimination, those whose rights are eroded in the name of national security, and human rights advocates who are targeted for defending the rights of others. These groups are often the first victims of societal instability and breakdown; their treatment is a harbinger of wider-scale repression. Human Rights First works to prevent violations against these groups and to seek justice and accountability for violations against them.

Human Rights First is practical and effective. We advocate for change at the highest levels of national and international policymaking. We seek justice through the courts. We raise awareness and understanding through the media. We build coalitions among those with divergent views. And we mobilize people to act.

Human Rights First is a nonprofit, nonpartisan international human rights organization based in New York and Washington D.C. To maintain our independence, we accept no government funding.

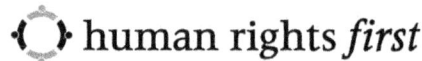

Acknowledgements

This report was written by Anwen Hughes and edited by Eleanor Acer. Additional editing was provided by Tad Stahnke, Annie Sovcik and Ruthie Epstein. We thank Sarah Graham for her work designing the report.

We wish to thank the many refugees and asylum seekers, attorneys, refugee services organizations and other community groups, Department of Homeland Security officials, and others who provided information included in this report.

About This Report

Information on refugees and asylum seekers affected by the immigration law's "terrorism bars" has been obtained from refugees and asylum seekers themselves, from their legal representatives, from decisions of the U.S. immigration courts, the Board of Immigration Appeals, and the federal courts of appeals, and from briefs filed in litigation by the Department of Homeland Security and the Department of Justice. Many of the names of the refugees and asylum seekers profiled in this report have been changed at their request. Due to fears for the safety of family members who remain in their home countries and the danger that could face those mistakenly labeled as "terrorists," privacy concerns surrounding the details of their past persecution, and concerns about jeopardizing their employment in the United States, these refugees have asked that their names be maintained in confidence.

{ }‣ human rights *first*

Headquarters

333 Seventh Avenue
13th Floor
New York, NY 10001-5108

Tel.: 212.845.5200
Fax: 212.845.5299

www.humanrightsfirst.org

Washington D.C. Office

100 Maryland Avenue, NE
Suite 500
Washington, DC 20002-5625

Tel: 202.547.5692
Fax: 202.543.5999

COVER PHOTOS (clockwise from top left)
Andrew Heavens / Reuters
STR New / Reuters
Rashid Talukder/Autograph ABP
Reuters Photographer / Reuters

Table of Contents

1. Summary and Recommendations

The Impact of the Immigration Law's "Terrorism Bars" on Asylum Seekers and Refugees in the United States

"You testified in your interview for Asylum that you were a member of one of the political factions fighting the Taliban in Afghanistan."

> Reason given by the U.S. Department of Homeland Security for denying permanent residence under the "terrorism bars" to an Afghan refugee (2008)

IMMIGRATION LAWS that target individuals who have engaged in or supported the commission of terrorist acts serve two very legitimate goals: to exclude from the United States people who threaten our national security, and to penalize people who have engaged in or supported acts of violence that are inherently wrongful and condemned under U.S. and international law. Both of these purposes are consistent with the United States' commitment to protect refugees who have fled political, religious and other forms of persecution. Indeed, the 1951 Refugee Convention and its Protocol explicitly exclude from protection persons who have committed a range of serious crimes, including acts of terrorism. The Refugee Convention also allows a country to expel a refugee who poses a danger to its security, or who has been convicted of a particularly serious crime in that country and constitutes a danger to the community.

But over the past eight years, thousands of legitimate refugees who pose no threat to the United States have had their applications for asylum, permanent residence, and family reunification denied or delayed due to overly broad provisions of U.S. immigration law that were intended to protect the United States against terrorism. Changes to the immigration laws as part of the USA PATRIOT Act in 2001 and the REAL ID Act in 2005 greatly expanded provisions relating to "terrorism." The enactment of these new provisions also

drew attention to the longstanding overbreadth of the immigration law's pre-existing definition of "terrorist activity."

Under these new and old laws, as they have been expansively interpreted by the federal agencies charged with enforcing them, refugees who were victimized by armed groups, including by groups the U.S. has officially designated as terrorist organizations, are being treated as "terrorists" themselves. Any refugee who ever fought against the military forces of an established government is being deemed a "terrorist." The fact that some of these refugees were actually fighting alongside U.S. forces shows how far removed the immigration law's "terrorist" labels have become from actual national security concerns. Refugees who voluntarily helped any group that used armed force are suffering the same fate— regardless of who or what the group's targets were and regardless of whether the assistance the refugee provided had any logical connection to violence.

Over 18,000 refugees and asylum seekers have been directly affected by these provisions to date. Currently, over 7,500 cases pending before the Department of Homeland Security are on indefinite hold based on some actual or perceived issue relating to the immigration law's "terrorism"-related provisions. The overwhelming majority of these cases are applications for permanent residence or family reunification filed by people who were granted asylum or refugee status several years ago and have been living and working in the

United States since then. In fact, in order to keep a person's case on hold based on the immigration law's "terrorism bars," the Department of Homeland Security must believe that the person does *not* pose a danger to the United States–this is a requirement of the agency's "hold" policy.

In 2007, Congress attempted to address the impact of these provisions on a few groups of refugees through piecemeal statutory changes, and also broadened the discretionary authority of the Secretaries of State and Homeland Security to grant "waivers" to exempt individual refugees from the impact of these provisions. These changes were helpful to particular groups of refugees who benefited from the partial implementation of the government's expanded waiver authority.

But the failure to address the flawed definitions and legal interpretations at the root of this problem, and the reliance on a cumbersome and duplicative "waiver" process as the exclusive means of resolving their unintended effects, have left many refugees in limbo–labeled as "terrorists," threatened with deportation back to persecution, separated from their families, and in some cases detained for lengthy periods. The implementation of "waivers," whose positive impact has mainly benefited refugees overseas, has not kept pace with the growing backlog in the United States.

Human Rights First, which has continued to monitor the impact of the immigration law's "terrorism"-related provisions on asylum seekers and refugees, is regularly receiving new reports of asylum seekers and refugees who are being affected by these provisions. Some of these recent or ongoing examples include:

- A refugee from Burundi was detained for over 20 months in a succession of county jails because the U.S. Department of Homeland Security and the immigration judge who would otherwise have granted him asylum took the position that he had provided "material support" to a rebel group because armed rebels robbed him of four dollars and his lunch.

- A young girl kidnapped at age 12 by a rebel group in the Democratic Republic of the Congo, used as a child soldier, and later threatened for advocating against the use of children in armed conflict, has been unable to receive a grant of asylum, as her application has been on hold for over a year because she was forced to take part in armed conflict as a child.

- A man who fled political and religious persecution in Bangladesh has had his application for permanent residence placed on indefinite hold because he took part in his country's successful struggle for independence–in 1971.

- The minor children of members of the democratic opposition from Sudan who were granted asylum in the United States years ago have been prevented from becoming permanent residents because the peaceful political activities of their parents have been deemed to constitute "material support to a terrorist organization."

The Obama Administration inherited this situation nine months ago, and is reviewing the range of potential solutions. The Administration should avoid the temptation to continue to take a piecemeal approach to this problem. Unless the core problems with the law and its interpretation are addressed, many of the issues raised in this report will go unresolved. Refugees who seek asylum in this country will continue to risk delayed adjudications, prolonged separation from family, and deportation in violation of the Refugee Convention. Attempts to deal with the overbreadth of the "terrorism bars" through a waiver process will continue to swallow the time of senior officials at U.S. Citizenship & Immigration Services, Immigration & Customs Enforcement, the DHS Offices of General Counsel and Policy, the Executive Office for Immigration Review and other components of the Department of Justice, the Department of State, and the National Security Council. And there will be no end to the jarring contradictions–with historical reality and other law–that our immigration system's understanding of "terrorism" continues to generate on a daily basis.

A more effective approach would be to fix the underlying statutory definitions and agency legal positions that have created this problem. Not only would such an approach allow the protection of the victims of persecution who seek refuge in this county, it would also help to ensure that the United

States is no longer labeling medical professionals who treat the wounded, parents who pay ransom to their children's kidnappers, and refugees who engaged in or supported military action against regimes—from Saddam Hussein in Iraq to the oppressive military junta still in power in Burma—that had blocked peaceful avenues for political change, as "terrorists" or supporters of terrorism by virtue of those facts alone.

The specific recommendations outlined at the end of this summary would not compromise security. Rather, they would help focus the scope and application of the immigration law's "terrorism"-related provisions on the people Congress intended those provisions to target. Implementing these recommendations would also free administrative resources that for the past four years have been focused overwhelmingly on people who do not pose a threat to the United States—resources that would be better spent on those who do.

The Immigration Law's Overly Broad Definitions

"We also believe that the definitions of terrorist activity, terrorist organization, and what constitutes material support to a terrorist organization in the Immigration and Nationality Act (INA) were written so broadly and applied so expansively that thousands of refugees are being unjustly labeled as supporters of terrorist organizations or participants in terrorist activities. . . We urge the committee to re-examine these definitions and to consider altering them in a manner which preserves their intent to prevent actual terrorists from entering our country without harming those who are themselves victims of terror—refugees and asylum seekers."

> Cardinal Theodore McCarrick, testifying before the Senate Subcommittee on Immigration, Refugees, and Border Security, October 8, 2009

The Overly Broad Definition of "Terrorist Activity"

"[F]ighting against the Iraqi Regime [of Saddam Hussein] meets the definition of engaging in terrorist activity."

> Stated basis for DHS's denial of permanent residence to a refugee from Iraq (2008)

The immigration law's current definition of "terrorist activity" is so broad that it sweeps in people who are neither guilty of criminal wrongdoing nor a threat to the United States. This provision, which has been in place since 1990, defines terrorist activity to include any unlawful use of a weapon against persons or property, for any purpose other than mere personal monetary gain. A law that defines any military action against a dictatorial regime as "terrorism" is just as likely to ensnare the United States' friends as its enemies. Nor does this definition of terrorist activity target the kind of criminal wrongdoing the term "terrorism" typically describes. The immigration law's definition can be read to cover everyone from George Washington to survivors of the Warsaw Ghetto uprising. The definition has been used against modern-day refugees who fought alongside U.S. forces to overthrow Saddam Hussein.

Compounding the problem, several provisions included in the USA PATRIOT Act of 2001 created new definitions of "terrorist organizations" and of "material support" that were based on this already overbroad definition of "terrorist activity." These amendments, which were further expanded in 2005 with the passage of the REAL ID Act, have dramatically extended the reach of the immigration law's original definition of "terrorist activity."

The "Tier III" Embarrassment: "Undesignated" Terrorist Organizations

"[O]ur own history is based on an armed response to a government that we could not change democratically."

> Immigration judge in *Matter of S-K*, expressing concern at breadth of the Tier III definition (2006)

The USA PATRIOT Act created a new and sweeping definition of a "terrorist organization" under the immigration laws. This three-part definition includes the "foreign terrorist organiza-tions" (commonly referred to as "Tier I" groups) that were designated as such by the Department of State under pre-existing provisions of law, as well as a second tier of organizations (commonly referred to as "Tier II" groups) that are also publicly listed as such by the Secretary of State. But it also includes a third category of groups, defined as "terrorist organizations" solely for purposes of the immigration laws. This third category includes "any group of two or more individuals, whether organized or not, which engages in, or has a subgroup which engages in" acts that the immigration law defines as "terrorist activity"—essentially, any unlawful use of a weapon for purposes other than personal enrich-ment. These groups are commonly referred to as "Tier III" or "undesignated" terrorist organizations.

In 2006, the U.S. Board of Immigration Appeals, in a case involving a Baptist member of a Burmese ethnic minority who had contributed to the Chin National Front, a group that fought the Burmese military junta, held that the targets and possible justifications of such use of force are legally irrelevant. The result of this holding is that the "Tier III terrorist organization" definition will apply to a group that has used force in self-defense against the army of a military regime that does not allow its citizens to change their government by peaceful means.

The immigration law's prohibition of "material support" to a "terrorist organization" makes anyone who contributes "material support" to a group liable for the worst acts of the group. The USA PATRIOT Act and subsequent amendments by the REAL ID Act also expanded the concept of "material support" to cover contributions not only to listed or desig-nated "Tier I" or "Tier II" organizations, but to any group deemed to meet the new "Tier III" definition. These changes to the immigration laws also made a broad range of other associations with these groups bars to refugee protection, permanent residence, and admission to the United States.

The result has been to label as "terrorist" an ever-expanding range of individuals and groups who pose no threat to the United States and have not engaged in any conduct that would be considered criminal under international law. Many of these refugees have been unjustly targeted by the immigration law's "terrorism"-related provisions due to their affiliation with groups that were U.S. allies or whose objectives the United States supports. For example:

- Saman Kareem Ahmad, an Iraqi former interpreter, now language and culture instructor, for the U.S. Marine Corps, was informed that his past connection to a Kurd-ish group allied with the United States made him inadmissible because the group was considered a "Tier III terrorist organization" under the immigration law. He was only granted a waiver of inadmissibility after he was profiled on the front page of the *Washington Post* in March 2008.

- Meanwhile, another member of Iraq's Kurdish ethnic minority who likewise served as an interpreter to U.S. forces in Iraq was also deemed inadmissible based on a past connection to the same Kurdish group that immi-gration adjudicators have concluded is a "Tier III terrorist organization." Unlike Saman Kareem, this former U.S. interpreter still has not been granted a waiver. The only obvious difference between the two cases is that this second man has been unable to publicize his situation due to fears for the safety of his family still in Iraq. While this second interpreter should benefit from the recent announcement of discretionary "waivers" for voluntary associations with the Kurdish group in question, the underlying problem of the Tier III definition remains. And the fact that this man has been left in limbo for a year and a half longer than his colleague shows how discre-tionary "waiver" authority that had been touted as a tool for flexibility has instead acted as a straitjacket.

- Multiple members of the Movement for Democratic Change (MDC), the main democratic opposition party in Zimbabwe, which has been on the receiving end of po-litical violence in that country, had their applications for permanent residence placed on hold or were informed that the U.S. Department of Homeland Security was considering terminating their asylum status because it considered the MDC to be a "Tier III terrorist organiza-tion." At the same time, in June 2009, President Obama was meeting with MDC leader Morgan Tsvangirai, cur-rently Prime Minister of Zimbabwe, and expressing his "extraordinary admiration" for Tsvangirai's "courage and tenacity" in navigating the very difficult political situation in his country.

While the Department of Homeland Security is reviewing some of its more outlandish "Tier III" characterizations (the MDC included), the fundamental problem is the "Tier III terrorist organization" definition itself, which will inevitably result in similar embarrassments in the future. In contrast to the other categories of "terrorist organizations" that are publicly designated as such on lists posted on the website of the U.S. Department of State, this new undesignated "Tier III" category is not listed anywhere. Groups that have been characterized as "terrorist organizations" under the immigration law's "Tier III" definition—and which the U.S. government does not consider "terrorist organizations" in any other context—include:

- All Iraqis, and Iraqi groups, who rose up against Saddam Hussein in the 1990's, including those who took part in the failed uprising at the end of the Gulf War of 1991 that was encouraged by the first President Bush;

- All Iraqis, and Iraqi groups, that later fought against Saddam Hussein's armies in conjunction with the Coalition forces that ultimately overthrew his regime in 2003;

- All of the Afghan *mujahidin* groups that fought the Soviet invasion in the 1980's, with U.S. support;

- The Democratic Unionist Party and the Ummah Party, two of the largest democratic opposition parties in Sudan, many of whose members were forced to flee the country in the years after the 1989 military coup that brought current President Omar Al-Bashir to power;

- The Sudan People's Liberation Movement/Army (SPLM/SPLA), the South Sudanese armed opposition movement that after years of civil war in pursuit of southern self-determination is now the ruling party of an autonomous Government of South Sudan;

- Virtually all Ethiopian and Eritrean political parties and movements, past and present;

- Every group ever to have fought the ruling military junta in Burma that was not included in the legislation that removed the Chin National Front and others from the scope of the Tier III definition;

- Any group that has used armed force against the regime in Iran since the 1979 revolution;

- The Movement for Democratic Change (MDC), the main political opposition to President Robert Mugabe of Zimbabwe.

This is not to say that an individual's activities in connection with these groups are irrelevant to a decision about that individual's eligibility for refugee protection or residence in the United States. But any activities that would be a legitimate basis for excluding a person are already covered by other provisions of the immigration law that do not rely on the overly broad "Tier III" definition.

The number of groups being characterized as "undesignated terrorist organizations" is growing daily, invisible to the public eye. Human Rights First receives regular inquiries from immigration lawyers and refugee advocates as to whether a particular organization "is a Tier III group." The problem with the Tier III definition is that there is no answer to that question. A group "is a Tier III group" when some immigration adjudicator, somewhere, says that it is, in the context of an individual case. And when that happens, there is no public announcement.

Attempts to implement "waivers" of the immigration law provisions relating to "Tier III" groups have been highly centralized and controlled, and have failed to keep pace with the completely decentralized process by which these groups are characterized as "undesignated terrorist organizations." While prompt implementation of an individualized waiver process for persons affected by this overbroad law is urgent and necessary, the "Tier III" definition will continue to create unnecessary suffering and embarrassment.

Targeting Refugees Rather Than Terrorists

"Our laws call on the Secretary of State to designate certain groups as terrorist groups. Other groups take up arms to resist tyrannical regimes, just as our founding fathers engaged in armed resistance to a relatively benign despotism. While we have been told that the current law does not allow such distinctions, there must be a way to distinguish between genuine terrorists and legitimate resistance groups. If current law does not do so, then we need to fix it."

> Rep. Chris Smith, hearing before the House Subcommittee on Africa, Global Human Rights and International Operations, Committee on International Relations, May 10, 2006

The government does not need the provisions of the immigration law that build on the "Tier III terrorist organization" definition as the basis to deport people it actually seeks to expel for security reasons. The immigration law allows the deportation or denial of entry to non-citizens based on a very broad range of human rights violations and common crimes. It also makes people lawfully admitted to this country deportable for reasons ranging from failing to maintain their visa status to failing to register a change of address.

The overly broad "terrorism"-related provisions of the immigration law are also bars to asylum or refugee resettlement for refugees currently seeking protection from persecution. But here too, the "Tier III" definition provides no additional security benefits, because other parts of the law already bar relief for anyone who poses a threat to the security of the United States or is guilty of acts of terrorism or other serious crimes. Indeed, U.S. law has long barred from both asylum and withholding of removal:

- People who engaged in or assisted in or incited the persecution of others;

- People who have been convicted of a particularly serious crime in the United States or have committed a serious non-political crime abroad;

- People who have engaged in terrorist activity (as noted above, the current definition of this term is overbroad, but a narrower definition would have a proper place in immigration enforcement and be consistent with U.S. commitments to refugee protection);

- People who are representatives of foreign terrorist organizations; or

- People who otherwise pose a threat to the security of the United States.

Moreover, refugees seeking resettlement from overseas, and refugees and asylees applying for permanent residence after their arrival, can be denied based on provisions of the immigration law that bar from the United States:

- People who are believed to be seeking to enter the U.S. to engage in unlawful activity;

- People whose entry or proposed activities in the United States the Secretary of State believes would have potentially serious adverse foreign policy consequences for the United States;

- People who have been members or affiliates of a totalitarian party;

- People who have been involved in genocide, torture, or extrajudicial killings;

- People who have been associated with a terrorist organization and intend to engage in activities in the United States that could endanger the welfare, safety, or security of the United States;

- People who are believed to have trafficked in controlled substances or colluded with others in doing so;

- People who admit having committed a crime involving moral turpitude;

- People who have sought to procure a visa or other immigration benefit or admission to the United States through fraud or willful misrepresentation of a material fact;

- People who have encouraged or assisted another person in trying to enter the U.S. illegally; as well as

■ People who have voted in violation of any Federal, State, or local law, have engaged in prostitution, have engaged or assisted in international child abduction, or are coming to the United States to practice polygamy.

Extreme and Inflexible Legal Positions

Over the last five years of the Bush Administration, the Departments of Homeland Security and Justice adopted interpretations of the immigration law's "terrorism"-related provisions that are extreme, inflexible, and inconsistent with this country's commitments under the Refugee Convention and Protocol. These legal positions have greatly exacerbated the impact of these terrorism-related provisions on legitimate refugees who were never their intended targets. These overly expansive legal positions include:

■ Treating victims of armed groups as supporters of the very groups that extorted goods or services from them under threat of violence;

■ Applying the "terrorism bars" to the acts of children in the same way as to adults, and as a result, barring a number of former child soldiers and child captives of armed groups;

■ Treating minimal contributions—a few dollars, a chicken, a bag of rice—as "material support;"

■ Interpreting "material support" to cover virtually anything, including non-violent speech and other purely political activity—e.g. writing for a student newspaper or distributing political flyers—that a person did in connection with his or her membership in a group the Department of Homeland Security deems to be a "terrorist organization" under the immigration laws, including a "Tier III" group;

■ Treating medical care as "material support;" and

■ Retroactive application of the USA PATRIOT Act's definition of a "Tier III" organization to groups that no longer exist or that have given up violence, stretching back as far as four decades.

Unfortunately, the Department of Homeland Security under the Obama Administration has thus far not altered the legal positions it inherited from its predecessors. These same positions continue to be adopted by immigration judges and the Board of Immigration Appeals in some individual cases. The Department of Homeland Security continues to use the "terrorism"-related provisions of the immigration law in a very expansive way to exclude refugees from protection or permanent residence, ironically based on the same facts these refugees themselves voluntarily disclosed to the U.S. government in making their claims for asylum or refugee protection. For example:

■ The asylum application of a woman from Ethiopia has been on hold for over three years because she took food to her son when he was arbitrarily detained for political reasons in a jail where prisoners were not fed. The son was involved in the political wing of a group DHS considers to be a "Tier III terrorist organization." But the mother was not, nor had she ever supported the group in any tangible way.

■ A young man who was granted asylum after fleeing persecution in Afghanistan over 20 years ago has yet to be granted permanent residence because he carried supplies as a child for a *mujahidin* group fighting the Soviet invasion in the 1980's. His childhood actions have been deemed "material support to a terrorist organization" under the USA PATRIOT Act. The *mujahidin* group in question dissolved years ago, and its former leaders have been key U.S. allies in post-Taliban Afghanistan.

The "Waiver" Process—Cumbersome and Inadequate

"[I]n my position I have responsibility for literally every policy matter that comes across the Department's plate, ranging from immigration and refugees to border screening and preparedness. And I personally have spent more time on this issue than on any other by far in volume, and that will continue to be the case, I think, until this issue is finally resolved."

> Paul Rosenzweig, Deputy Asst. Secretary for Policy, U.S. Department of Homeland Security, September 19, 2007

Since 2006, the Executive Branch has openly acknowledged that the immigration law's "terrorism bars" are having an unintended impact on refugees, and that this is a problem. Rather than rethink their interpretation of some of these provisions and support legislation to correct the underlying legal definitions, the immigration agencies insisted that the sole solution was for them to grant discretionary "waivers" to individual applicants. This power has been vested by Congress in the Secretary of Homeland Security and the Secretary of State, in consultation with the Attorney General.

But attempts to fully implement this discretionary authority, enacted in 2005 and expanded in 2007, have fallen victim to unprecedented levels of official paralysis, while the number of refugees suffering from the impact of these provisions continues to grow. Attempts by the Secretary of Homeland Security, the Secretary of State, and the Attorney General to implement the statutory waiver authority have shown why a process that requires consultation among three Cabinet-level officials is not a realistic method of conducting refugee status determinations and other routine immigration adjudications. Discussions over basic frameworks to implement waiver authority have required protracted negotiation among very high-level government officials who also have many other urgent claims on their time. Granting waivers related to particular "Tier III" groups—some of them so long defunct that their consideration has required archival research—has likewise foundered, as the debate over whether or not to grant a group-based waiver becomes a referendum on the group that is often quite disconnected from the facts and equities of the individual asylum seekers and refugees affected.

Where waivers have been implemented, the Department of Homeland Security has been approving cases. Since implementation began in late 2006, waivers have been granted in 8,961 refugee cases overseas, 1,821 applications for permanent residence and family reunification filed by refugees and asylees already granted protection, and 253 asylum seekers whose affirmative applications for asylum were pending before the Department of Homeland Security's Asylum Office. But these cases have only been approved after two levels of often duplicative adjudication, first on the merits of the application for asylum or other status, and then on whether or not to grant a waiver. Applicants are given no clear information about what is happening to their cases and those who are granted a waiver receive no notice of this fact. This opaque and often duplicative process results in significant delay, and provides no opportunity to appeal a mistaken decision. Some cases in immigration court are not being considered for waivers at all, while those that are considered face extraordinary delays.

The Department of Homeland Security and the Department of State should make progress toward full implementation of discretionary waiver authority an urgent priority. The experience of the past four years, however, has confirmed that waivers cannot be the exclusive means of addressing the overbreadth of the "terrorism bars." Legislative change is needed to ensure that refugees can have their cases decided effectively and without delay, with essential safeguards like the opportunity to appeal a mistaken decision. Legislative change would also allow these federal agencies to focus their application of the immigration law's "terrorism"-related provisions on those Congress intended to target.

More Progress Needed on "Duress" Waivers

The Departments of State and Homeland Security have now finally implemented their authority to grant exceptions to the "material support" bar to applicants who were forced to give goods or services to all categories of armed groups. The implementation of these waivers in cases pending before the Department of Homeland Security is making an enormous difference to the individual refugees affected. Nearly all the asylum seekers who have been granted waivers of any of the immigration law's "terrorism bars" since waiver implementation within the United States began in 2007 have been duress cases.

But implementation of duress waivers has extended only to the "material support" bar, leaving out equally deserving refugees whose victimization fell under some other legal heading. Several child soldiers who fled to the United States in search of refuge are among those caught in this gap in waiver implementation, because they were actually sent into combat or received "military-type training" from their captors. Moreover, as discussed below, refugees otherwise eligible for a duress waiver of the "material support" bar who are in immigration court proceedings—rather than before the Asylum Office—face years of delay before they can be considered for relief.

Still No Waivers for Voluntary Support to "Tier III" Groups

"I recognize that the waiver authority Congress provided to the executive branch resulted in some positive changes in recent months. The executive branch is granting waivers to those whose 'support' under the overly broad definition of terrorist organization was provided only under duress. Some others, whose support was provided to groups exempt from the definition of terrorist organization, are also being granted protection. But that is not enough. The third tier of the law's definition of terrorist organization continues to ensnare those deserving of our protection who pose no legitimate threat to the United States."

> Sen. Patrick Leahy, statement for the Congressional Record, August 5, 2009

Meanwhile, refugees whose legal problems stem from a *voluntary* connection to any non-governmental group that used armed force—a potential "Tier III" group—remain in limbo or worse. Despite three years of active discussion at

the highest levels of government, and of bipartisan Congressional concern, no comprehensive "waivers" have been implemented for voluntary associations with or support to groups that are now considered "Tier III terrorist organizations" for purposes of U.S. immigration law.

Attempts to implement this waiver authority on a group-by-group basis (i.e. by issuing announcements specific to associations with particular "Tier III" groups) have proved unworkable. In 2007, waivers were announced for "material support" to 10 named groups, many of whose members and supporters were slated for resettlement in the United States as refugees at about the same time the "terrorism bar problem" nearly shut down the U.S. resettlement program in 2006. Those 10 waivers, while helpful to the immediate needs of the U.S. refugee resettlement program and of several populations of refugees stranded overseas, had minimal impact on the asylum seekers, asylees, and refugees already in the United States who are the focus of this report. The 10 groups in question were later removed from the "Tier III" definition by the passage of legislation in late 2007; waivers were subsequently extended for people who had been combatants with those same groups or had other connections to them that barred them from protection in the United States.

The only group-based measure implemented since then has been the very recent announcement of waivers for persons associated with three Iraqi groups: the Iraqi National Congress, the Patriotic Union of Kurdistan, and the Kurdish Democratic Party. These waivers had been under discussion since the spring of 2008. This group-based approach leaves refugees associated with all other groups without relief, however non-violent their own activities may have been and however great their need.

- An Oromo woman from Ethiopia, for example, was granted asylum several years ago based on the persecution she suffered there due to her peaceful activities as a member of the Oromo Liberation Front (OLF). For those activities she was jailed without charges by Ethiopian security forces, and was beaten, whipped, and stomped on. She was also raped by one of her interrogators. She believes it was as a result of this rape that she became infected with HIV, as her husband was HIV-negative. In early 2008, this woman was denied permanent residence based on the same political activities she had described in her application for asylum. Her daughter, still a minor, received a denial letter stating: "You are the child of an inadmissible alien. For that reason, you are inadmissible . . . " The family's applications were later reopened, but due to the lack of waiver implementation for voluntary association with groups like the OLF that are considered "Tier III" organizations, they remain on hold a year and a half later.

While U.S. government officials have indicated that they are currently assessing implementation of additional aspects of their discretionary "waiver" authority, the continuing lack of a "waiver" for voluntary associations and activities that should not bar a person from refugee protection or subsequent integration is an urgent problem. Applicants for asylum or permanent residence who were involved in straightforward political activities in connection with groups the U.S. government does not treat as "terrorist organizations" in any other context face years of delay, and in some cases the threat of deportation. The lack of resolution of this problem also limits the ability of the U.S. government to resettle other refugee populations currently trapped in very difficult or dangerous situations overseas. And it causes regular public embarrassment as U.S. immigration law continues to define as "terrorist" numerous groups that do not merit this characterization and that the United States government actually supports.

The Immigration Court Waiver Process

"[C]ases involving material support provided to [Tier III] terrorist organizations are on hold with USCIS. However, the ICE/OPLA directive is to move forward with cases such as the respondent's. As the respondent is not eligible for any of the exemptions in place at this time . . . there is no reason to continue this case indefinitely."

Court filing by DHS Immigration & Customs Enforcement, urging immigration court not to delay deportation of Ethiopian asylum seeker (October 2009)

For asylum seekers and others in immigration court proceedings, waivers (whether based on duress or other grounds) are simply not working. It took the Department of Homeland Security over three years from the time its statutory waiver authority was enacted in 2005 to devise a process to implement that authority in immigration court cases. And that process, finally implemented in late 2008, has proved so constricted in its scope, and so flawed in its implementation, that as of September 2009 it had led to the consideration of only a handful of cases nationwide. Asylum seekers who are actually facing deportation to countries where they would face persecution—and who thus have the most compelling and urgent of claims to the United States' treaty obligations towards them—continue to face the greatest obstacles in even being considered for those waivers that have already been implemented, and to receive the lowest degree of government protection.

The key flaws in the immigration court waiver process are that (1) it does not provide for waiver consideration until the applicant has already been ordered deported and that order is considered administratively "final," resulting in years of unnecessary delay and, in some cases, prolonged detention, as well as significant expense to the government; (2) it does not apply to the unknown number of cases denied based on the "terrorism bars" between October 2001 and September 2008, unless and until the applicant is detained; (3) it provides no protection against actual deportation for people for whom the Department of Homeland Security has not yet implemented waivers—individuals in this situation whose applications for asylum are being adjudicated by the Department of Homeland Security are placed "on hold" pending waiver implementation, but those whose applications for asylum are adjudicated by the immigration courts are not. These defects are having a serious impact on asylum applicants whose cases have been before the immigration courts. For example:

■ A young man from Somalia who fled to the United States seeking protection from a militant group that had kidnapped him has been detained in a U.S. immigration jail for over a year, and will likely remain detained for the duration of his administrative appeal, because he does not have a final order of deportation. The immigration judge, who found him credible, explicitly recommended that he be granted a waiver of the "material support" bar, but the process the Department of Homeland Security has put in place to do this does not consider a person's case until administrative appeals are abandoned or exhausted. It does not appear from the facts of this man's case that the "material support" bar should actually apply (as he did nothing to assist the militants), but while he litigates this point, he remains in jail.

■ A woman who applied for asylum from political persecution in Eritrea, and whose testimony was found to be credible, was denied all relief by an immigration judge based on the fact that she had provided support, in the late 1970's, to a group then fighting for Eritrea's independence from Ethiopia. Ethiopia at that time was ruled by the notoriously brutal Dergue regime, which jailed this woman and subjected her to repeated torture. Because he found that she was barred from asylum based on the "terrorism bars," the immigration judge did not decide whether the woman was otherwise statutorily eligible for refugee protection. The Board of Immigration Appeals agreed that the "terrorism bars" applied. This asylum applicant's appeal is currently pending before the federal court of appeals. If the court of appeals denies her appeal based on the "terrorism bars," this woman could be deported without ever having received a decision on the merits of her asylum claim and without ever having been considered for a waiver.

The U.S. government does not know how many refugees who have sought asylum before the immigration courts since 2001 have had their cases denied or delayed due to the immigration law's sweeping "terrorism"-related bars. Neither the Department of Justice, which includes the immigration courts, nor DHS's Immigration & Customs Enforcement (ICE), whose lawyers represent DHS in those courts, has tracked the number of persons seeking asylum in the immigration courts who have been denied asylum on this basis to date.

The Consequences: Divided Families, Lengthy Detentions and Delayed Integration

Refugees wrongly classified as "terrorists" or supporters of "terrorism" under the immigration law's overbroad definitions continue to suffer severe practical consequences. Those who have already been granted asylum or refugee protection here are unable to reunite with their spouses and children who remain in what are often very difficult or dangerous situations abroad. For example:

■ A mother from Cameroon was granted asylum based on her peaceful political activism for the rights of Cameroon's English-speaking minority. Her petition to bring her children to join her in the U.S. was placed on hold based on DHS's determination that the Southern Cameroons National Council (SCNC) should be considered a "Tier III" group. By the time DHS indicated it was reconsidering its assessment of the SCNC, one of her children had died of natural causes.

Others whose applications for protection are pending before the immigration courts can face prolonged detention. Human Rights First is aware of cases of refugees who have been detained for one or two years or more while they awaited resolution of an alleged "terrorism bar." For example:

■ A Sri Lankan refugee who paid ransom to his own kidnappers still has not received a waiver of the "material support" bar after nearly five years in immigration proceedings. As a result he has remained separated from his wife even as conditions in their home country deteriorated dramatically. He himself spent the first two and a half years of his time in the United States in immigration detention, and now, two years after his release from those jail-like conditions, is still forced to wear a large, uncomfortable, and humiliating ankle bracelet.

For all those affected, these legal obstacles delay the full integration into the U.S. community that they all need and that many of these refugees have been working towards for years. Young people whose asylum applications are on hold are ineligible for the financial aid that would enable them to pursue higher education. Refugees with professional qualifications have seen job offers withdrawn because they lack permanent residence. Elderly and disabled persons have faced interruptions in their medical coverage for the same reason.

A Way Forward

After eight years of legislative expansion and expansive interpretation, the immigration law's "terrorism"-related provisions continue to be used to deny or delay protection or permanent status to refugees who pose no threat to the security of the United States. In virtually all of these cases, the problems these refugees are facing under the "terrorism bars" stem from facts they themselves voluntarily described to the United States government in their applications for protection. In the largest number of the cases currently "on hold" with the Department of Homeland Security, the refugees in question were already granted asylum or refugee protection after disclosure of—and often based on—those same facts.

More than four years after discretionary "waiver" authority was enacted in 2005, the "waiver" approach has proved inadequate as the primary means of resolving these cases, and legislative tinkering in 2007 to address the needs of individual refugee groups has left others—refugees who are equally deserving—without relief. It is past time for the United States to bring its laws and administrative procedures back into line with its treaty obligations to protect refugees and with the U.S. tradition of extending protection to those who flee from persecution.

Congress and the Administration must take a thorough and even-handed approach to address the roots of this problem. Specific recommendations for both Congress and the Administration are outlined below. These changes are critical in order to ensure that the immigration law's "terrorism bars"—consistently with U.S. treaty obligations—target those who actually bear responsibility for serious wrongdoing or pose a threat to the security of the United States. They are also necessary so that legitimate refugees who seek asylum

in this country are not left to suffer continued delays in adjudication, prolonged detention or separation from family, and possible deportation in violation of the Refugee Convention. These changes will also help to ensure that the United States is no longer labeling physicians who treat the wounded, victims of armed groups, and even its own founding fathers and its soldiers abroad, as "terrorists" or supporters of "terrorism."

None of the targeted reforms described below would undermine national security. They would not affect the bars to refugee protection for anyone who is a threat to the security of the United States or who has persecuted other people or committed other serious crimes, including terrorist acts. Nor would these measures change the law's expansive provisions that bar the entry, or allow the deportation, of non-citizens on a wide range of other grounds ranging from criminal activity to civil violations of immigration rules.

Recommendations to Congress

■ Eliminate the statutory concept of a "Tier III" terrorist organization, which has led to numerous unintended consequences but is not needed as an enforcement tool against its intended targets. Individuals culpable of wrongdoing are captured by the other provisions of the immigration law that allow a person to be excluded or deported from the United States (including provisions based on support to "Tier I" and "Tier II" organizations, which would be unaffected by this change). Individuals who pose a threat to the security of the United States or are believed to be coming here for unlawful purposes would likewise be covered by other existing provisions of the law.

■ Amend the immigration law's definition of "terrorist activity" (currently understood to cover any unlawful use of armed force by a non-state actor, against anyone and anything) so that it (a) targets only the use of violence for purposes of intimidation or coercion (of a civilian population or of a government or an international organi-zation), and (b) no longer applies to uses of armed force that would not be unlawful under international humanitarian law.

- If the relevant federal agencies continue to apply the "material support" bar to involuntary conduct, amend the immigration law's definition of "material support" to make clear that it does not apply to acts done under coercion.

- Eliminate the provision that makes a person inadmissible simply for being the spouse or child of a person inadmissible under the immigration law's "terrorism"-related grounds.

- Allow waiver decisions to be made at the same time the case as a whole is decided by the immigration court, by giving waiver authority to the Attorney General for cases pending before the Department of Justice, with the provision that the Attorney General delegate this authority to the immigration courts.

Recommendations to the Departments of Homeland Security, Justice, and State

(1) Support Statutory Reform

- Support the statutory amendments outlined in the recommendations to Congress above.

(2) Interpret Existing Law Consistently with Its Text and Purpose, to Target Those Who Advance Terrorist Activity

- Stop applying the "terrorism bars" to involuntary conduct and other circumstances where the common law would recognize a defense (e.g. the acts of children).

- Stop interpreting "material support" to apply to contributions of goods or services that are insignificant and/or bear no logical connection to the furtherance of terrorist activity.

- Stop applying the Tier III definition to defunct groups and groups that have given up violence. Individuals who were themselves responsible for criminal acts of violence, or who presently pose a threat to the security of the United States, would still be barred under other provisions of law.

- Confirm that a group was actually engaged in violence during the periods of time relevant to individual cases, and that any violent activities were authorized by the group, before a group is deemed to be a "Tier III terrorist organization." (A failure to do this probably accounts for the sudden classification as "Tier III" groups of the Nepali Congress Party and Zimbabwe's Movement for Democratic Change.)

- Define a larger group as a "Tier III terrorist organization" based on the actions of a subset of its members only in cases where the subgroup is actually an integral part of a larger group and operates under the direction of the larger group. This will help avoid labeling peaceful political parties as "Tier III" groups because they form coalitions with other groups that include armed wings.

(3) A More Effective and Fair Approach to Waivers

- Authorize waivers for voluntary conduct in connection with a Tier III group that allow for an individualized assessment along the lines of the existing duress waiver.

- Authorize waivers in connection with later-filed applications (e.g. permanent residence and family reunification) filed by any person previously granted status or relief from removal in the United States, where the activities or associations that are now leading the person to be seen as inadmissible or deportable were disclosed in the application or proceeding that led to the prior grant of status or relief, there is no reason to believe the person poses a danger to the safety and security of the United States, and the person has undergone and passed relevant background and security checks.

- Authorize waivers for bars other than the "material support" bar in cases where the conduct giving rise to the bar was coerced.

- Until such time as the statute is changed to eliminate inadmissibility based solely on spousal or filial relationships, authorize waivers for spouses and children being affected solely by these provisions.

- As long as DHS retains waiver authority in immigration court cases, allow such authority to be exercised as soon as the person is found to be eligible for relief but for a "terrorism bar" and that finding is final.

- As long as DHS retains waiver authority in immigration court cases, ensure that persons in immigration court proceedings for whom DHS has not yet implemented waivers are not deported before implementation happens, by requiring that all removal cases subject to a "terrorism bar" and otherwise eligible for relief are forwarded by ICE to USCIS for waiver consideration.

2. Protecting Refugees While Excluding Criminals and Dangerous People—The Proper Function of the Immigration Law's "Terrorism Bars"

IN THE AFTERMATH of World War II, the United States played a leading role in building an international system for the protection of refugees, to ensure that the nations of the world would never again refuse to offer shelter to people fleeing persecution. The United States has committed to the central guarantees of the 1951 Refugee Convention and its 1967 Protocol.[1] The United States passed the Refugee Act of 1980 in order to bring our nation's laws into compliance with the Refugee Convention and Protocol.[2] That legislation incorporated into the Immigration and Nationality Act ("INA") provisions establishing the domestic asylum and refugee resettlement systems that in the years since then have helped over two million refugees escape persecution and begin new lives in this country.

U.S. and international law prohibit the return of a refugee to any country where his or her life or freedom would be threatened on account of his or her race, religion, nationality, membership in a particular social group, or political opinion. U.S. law allows persons present in the United States who can establish that they have suffered past persecution or have a well-founded fear of persecution on these grounds to be granted asylum as a discretionary measure. U.S. law prohibits the deportation of a refugee who can show that he or she would face a probability of persecution if deported. Refugees in this situation are entitled to the mandatory protection of "withholding of removal." In parallel to these measures to protect refugees within the United States, the U.S. government, in partnership with local communities and religious and other groups across the country, also resettles in the United States refugees overseas who have fled their home countries and have no prospect of return.

Consistent with provisions of the Refugee Convention that favor the integration of refugees into their host countries, the United States allows persons granted asylum (and requires resettled refugees) to apply for permanent residence a year after they are first granted protection. Permanent residence sets a refugee on the path to U.S. citizenship, and facilitates many other undertakings including finding a job and buying a home. U.S. law also allows asylees and refugees to petition for reunification with spouses or children who were not able to be granted asylum or refugee status together with them, typically because they were stranded in a different location overseas.

The Refugee Convention's requirements of protection are subject to exceptions, however: the Convention's "exclusion clauses" require host countries to exclude from its protections persons who have committed heinous acts or grave crimes that make them undeserving of international protection as refugees, even though they have a well-founded fear of persecution. A separate provision of the Convention allows the return of refugees who pose a danger to the security of the host country. The United States incorporated into its law the Refugee Convention's promise to provide protection to refugees, but also codified bars to asylum and withholding of removal intended to reflect the Convention's exceptions. These provisions prohibit granting any form of refugee protection to:

■ People who engaged in or assisted in or incited the persecution of others;

■ People who have been convicted of a particularly serious crime in the United States;

- People who have committed a serious non-political crime abroad;

- People who have engaged in terrorist activity;

- People who are representatives of foreign terrorist organizations; or

- People who otherwise pose a threat to the security of the United States.[3]

Refugees seeking resettlement from overseas, and refugees and asylees applying for permanent residence after their arrival, can be denied based on provisions of the immigration law that bar from United States:

- People who are believed to be seeking to enter the U.S. to engage in unlawful activity;

- People whose entry or proposed activities in the United States the Secretary of State believes would have potentially serious adverse foreign policy consequences for the United States;

- People who have been members or affiliates of a totalitarian party;

- People who have been involved in genocide, torture, or extrajudicial killings;

- People who have been associated with a terrorist organization and intend to engage in activities in the United States that could endanger the welfare, safety, or security of the United States;

- People who are believed to have trafficked in controlled substances or to have colluded with others in doing so;

- People who admit having committed a crime involving moral turpitude;

- People who have sought to procure a visa or other immigration benefit or admission to the United States through fraud or willful misrepresentation of a material fact;

- People who have encouraged or assisted another person in trying to enter the U.S. illegally; as well as

- People who have voted in violation of any Federal, State, or local law, have engaged in prostitution, have engaged or assisted in international child abduction, or are coming to the United States to practice polygamy.[4]

The purpose of the Refugee Convention's "exclusion clauses" and exceptions to the obligation not to return refugees to persecution was to ensure that perpetrators of heinous acts and serious crimes are identified and cannot use the refugee protection system to avoid being held accountable for their actions, and that refugees who threaten the safety of the community in their host countries can be removed. These are important and legitimate goals.[5] In order to be consistent with the Refugee Convention, however, exclusion from protection of a person who meets the refugee definition must be predicated on the individual refugee's individual responsibility for serious wrongdoing.[6] Either the refugee must have individually committed an excludable offense (which would include acts of terrorism as that term is commonly understood), or he or she must have contributed to its commission in a significant way, and have done so knowingly and voluntarily. Similarly, while the Refugee Convention allows the United States (like any other country that is a party to the Convention or Protocol) to deny protection to a refugee who poses a danger to the United States, this must be based on a finding that the refugee actually poses a danger.[7]

Unfortunately, the passage of the USA PATRIOT Act in 2001 and the REAL ID Act in 2005, combined with sudden attention, beginning in late 2004, to the longstanding overbreadth of the immigration law's definition of "terrorist activity," has turned these principles upside down. Under these new and old laws, as they are being expansively interpreted by the federal agencies charged with enforcing them, refugees who were victimized by armed groups, including groups the U.S. has designated as terrorist organizations, are being treated as terrorists themselves. Refugees who fought decades ago for the independence of countries now long recognized by the United States are being described as having "engaged in terrorist activity" for taking part in combat against an opposing army. Any refugee who ever fought against the military forces of an established government—including governments like that of Saddam

Hussein in Iraq that did not allow their citizens to change their government through peaceful means—is being deemed a terrorist. The fact that some of these refugees were actually fighting alongside U.S. forces shows how far removed the immigration law's "terrorist" labels have become from actual national security concerns. Refugees who voluntarily helped any group that used armed force are suffering the same fate— regardless of the circumstances in which that group used force, regardless of who or what its targets were, and regardless of whether the assistance the refugee provided had any logical connection to violence.

The result is that hundreds of asylum seekers over the past eight years have seen the protection they need denied or delayed, in some cases indefinitely, while thousands of refugees and asylees already granted protection are facing indefinite separation from stranded family members or are unable to achieve full integration into the communities where they have been living and working and raising families for as long as 20 years. How did our immigration system reach this point?

3. The Road to Absurdity—A Brief History of the "Terrorism"-Related Provisions of the Immigration & Nationality Act

"Congress, we assume, never meant to rewrite federal law so that victims of totalitarian regimes and those forced to serve human rights abusers are kept out of the United States. Yet an accumulation of legal changes in recent years, culminating in the REAL ID Act last year, has done just that."

Editorial, "Fix This Law," *Washington Post*, April 17, 2006

THE PRESENT CRISIS has its root in the U.S. immigration law's definition of "terrorist activity." This grossly overbroad definition has been on the books since 1990, but in the years since 2001, two things happened that have greatly magnified and extended its effects.

First, new provisions were added to the immigration laws that built on that overbroad definition of "terrorist activity." Most significant among them was the creation of a new category of "undesignated" terrorist organizations, and the prohibition of "material support," not only to listed or designated "terrorist organizations," but also to any group deemed to fall under the new "undesignated" rubric. (The current version of the relevant provisions of the immigration law appears as Appendix A to this report.)

Second, the Departments of Homeland Security and Justice adopted new and increasingly extreme interpretations both of that original definition of "terrorist activity" and of the new provisions relating to "material support" to "terrorist organizations." These interpretations, discussed in Part 4 of this report, were also applied to the refugee resettlement program administered by the U.S. Department of State, and to the other visa applications adjudicated by the State Department.

The Immigration Law's Definition of "Terrorist Activity"

"[V]ery, very broad."

> Jonathan Scharfen, Deputy Director, USCIS (March 2008) (describing the immigration law's definitions of "terrorist organization" and "activity")[8]

"[B]reathtaking in its scope."

> Juan P. Osuna, Acting Vice Chairman, Board of Immigration Appeals (June 2006) (describing same statutory language)[9]

The Immigration & Nationality Act (INA) defines "terrorist activity" to mean "any activity which is unlawful under the laws of the place where it is committed (or which, if it had been committed in the United States, would be unlawful under the laws of the United States or any State) and which involves" any one of a range of violent acts, including:

> "the use of any . . . explosive, firearm, or other weapon or dangerous device (other than for mere personal monetary gain), with intent to endanger, directly or indirectly, the safety of one or more individuals or to cause substantial damage to property."[10]

This definition was enacted as part of the Immigration Act of 1990.[11] Read literally (as indeed the Departments of Homeland Security and Justice are currently reading it), it covers virtually any use of armed force by a non-state actor, directed at anyone or anything, for any purpose other than personal enrichment. It thus sweeps in everyone from George Washington to Iraqi refugees who rose up against Saddam Hussein in 1991, with the encouragement of the first President Bush.

This definition also covers those individuals who make civilians and non-combatants targets of their violence— something that is universally illegitimate regardless of motive or circumstance. But as detailed in Part 2 of this report, numerous other provisions of the Immigration & Nationality Act exist to bar those people from the United States. The immigration law bars non-citizens from entry on a broad range of criminal grounds, for example, which courts have applied to offenses including (and by no means limited to) aggravated assault, kidnapping, carrying a concealed weapon with intent to use it, murder and voluntary manslaughter, robbery, terroristic threats, arson, blackmail, burglary, embezzlement, extortion, theft, illegal use of credit cards, counterfeiting, document fraud offenses, mail fraud, money laundering, obstruction of justice, perjury, and tax evasion. Persons believed to have been involved in drug trafficking will be denied entry on that basis. A person can also be denied entry if the Attorney General or a consular officer reasonably believes that he seeks to enter the United States to engage (solely, principally, or incidentally) in *any* unlawful activity. People already in the United States, including lawful permanent residents, can be deported if they were inadmissible at the time they were admitted to the country, if they have violated the conditions of their non-immigrant status, if they have been convicted after entry of a broad range of crimes including those mentioned above, or if at any time after being admitted to the United States they engage in any criminal activity which endangers public safety or national security. (The full range of statutory bars to refugee protection, and of the reasons that allow the government to deny a non-citizen entry to the United States, or to deport one who is already here, is reproduced in Appendix A.)

For years, however, the Justice Department (which at that time included both the former Immigration & Naturalization Service and the immigration court system) did not read the

"terrorist activity" definition in such an expansive way. In 1988, the Board of Immigration Appeals (BIA), the administrative appeals court that reviews the decisions of the immigration courts, had ruled that having taken part in military activity in the context of a civil war, whether on the government side or as part of a guerrilla force, did not constitute persecution of others such as to bar a person from refugee protection.[12] In 1990, the BIA considered the case of a young asylum seeker who had been targeted for arrest by the secret police in that country for aiding the *mujahidin* forces that were fighting the Afghan national army and its Soviet backers after the Soviet invasion of Afghanistan.[13] The secret police had arrested this young man's younger brother, who was apparently still a minor at the time and had not been seen since. The BIA granted the young man asylum, in a decision that was often cited as affirming a "right to rebel" against a government that does not allow its citizens to change their government through peaceful means. The BIA's decision also noted the abysmal human rights record of the regime in question, including State Department reports of widespread torture of political prisoners, thousands of whom were believed to be held in Afghanistan during that period.[14]

When the INA's definition of terrorist activity was enacted later that year (1990), it was understood consistently with these earlier precedents. In the years that followed, and even after having "engaged in terrorist activity" became a bar to all forms of refugee protection in 1996, people who had fought opposing military forces in similar circumstances were granted asylum or resettled in the United States as refugees.

The USA PATRIOT Act, the New Definition of "Terrorist Organization," and the Concept of "Material Support"

"The law bars as refugees people who have been members or supporters of any group with 'two or more individuals, whether organized or not, [which] engages in, or has as subgroup which engages in" activities as broad as using an "explosive, firearm or other weapon or dangerous device." The result has kept out the sort of people America's traditionally generous refugee policy was designed to help. . . Not every armed group is a terrorist organization; American policy should not treat victims of the worst sort of violence like perpetrators of it."

Editorial, "The Refugee Mess," *Washington Post*, October 24, 2006

The USA PATRIOT Act, enacted in the immediate aftermath of the events of September 11, 2001, expanded the "terrorism"-related provisions of the immigration law in two significant ways.

First, it added a definition of a "terrorist organization," consisting of three categories of armed groups.

Second, it defined "material support" to a "terrorist organization" in any of these three categories as "terrorist activity" in its own right. Because other provisions of the immigration law already barred anyone who had "engaged in terrorist activity" from all forms of refugee protection, these amendments greatly expanded the scope of the bars to asylum and withholding of removal.

The first two categories of "terrorist organizations" defined in the USA PATRIOT Act's three-part definition are those groups whose names appear on lists that are publicly available on the State Department's website. (The current version of these lists appears as Appendix B to this report.) These include groups designated as "foreign terrorist organizations" under section 219 of the INA (what are sometimes referred to as "Tier I" organizations), and organizations placed on the "Terrorism Exclusion List" by publication in the Federal Register (commonly referred to as "Tier II" organizations).

"Tier I" and "Tier II" groups include Al-Qaeda, the Shining Path (Peru), the FARC, ELN, and AUC (Colombia), the Basque ETA, the Communist Party of the Philippines/New People's Army, Hamas, Hizballah, the Armed Islamic Group or GIA (Algeria), the Abu Nidal Organization, the Abu Sayyaf Group, the Al-Aqsa Martyrs Brigade, the Liberation Tigers of Tamil Eelam (LTTE) (Sri Lanka), the Real IRA (Ireland/Northern Ireland), the Orange Volunteers (Northern Ireland), Lashkar-e Tayyiba (Pakistan/Kashmir), Al-Shabaab (Somalia), the Communist Party of Nepal (Maoist), the Japanese Red Army, the Revolutionary United Front (RUF) (Sierra Leone), the Lord's Resistance Army (LRA) (Uganda), and many others.

The third category of "terrorist organizations" defined by the USA PATRIOT Act, however, is not listed anywhere. This section of the definition describes as a "terrorist organization" any "group of two or more individuals, whether organized or not, which engages in, or has a subgroup which engages in" what the immigration law defines as "terrorist activity." (The "subgroup" language was added in 2005 by the REAL ID Act.) There is no requirement that such groups be listed or designated by any central authority, in any historical or political context, or based on any assessment that the group poses a risk of a kind that should be of concern to the U.S. government. The definition of a "Tier III" organization sets up no process for assessing who is being endangered by the "terrorist activity" of the group or its "subgroup," how serious that danger is, or whether such "terrorist activity" is a dominant characteristic of the activities of the group as a whole—all considerations that, explicitly or implicitly, enter into the designation or listing process applicable to Tiers I and II.

Immigration officials making decisions in individual asylum and refugee cases, for example, have in recent years been characterizing legal opposition parties in several different countries as "Tier III terrorist organizations" based on incidents of violence between some of their supporters and supporters of rival parties—rival parties which would also, by this logic, be Tier III organizations, leaving citizens of the countries in question few avenues for democratic participation that will not make them inadmissible to the United States. Parties affected by this characterization have ranged from the Awami League in Bangladesh to the Movement for Democratic Change in Zimbabwe. And in looking at groups that have actually engaged in armed conflict, the Board of Immigration Appeals has held that a group that only fought the soldiers of an opposing army, did not target civilians, and is acknowledged to pose no threat whatsoever to the United States, will nonetheless be considered a "Tier III terrorist organization."[15]

Groups are deemed to be "Tier III" terrorist organizations in an *ad hoc* fashion, in connection with a particular refugee applicant's case. There is no central control over the application of this definition, which is triggered simply by an individual adjudicator's assessment that the group or some subgroup within it has engaged in the use of armed force.

The USA PATRIOT Act did not invent the notion of "material support:" since 1990, providing "material support, including a safe house, transportation, communications, funds, false identification, weapons, explosives, or training to any individual the actors knows or has reason to believe has committed or plans to commit an act of terrorist activity" had made a person inadmissible to, and deportable from, the United States. Since 1996, "material support" (as just defined) had also been a bar to asylum in this country. The 1996 immigration law expanded this provision to include material support to a terrorist organization "in conducting a terrorist activity," but "terrorist organization," in this context, was understood to mean a "foreign terrorist organization" designated as such by the Secretary of State under section 219 of the INA (i.e. a "Tier I" organization). Provision of material support to these organizations was (and is) also a crime for both U.S. citizens and non-citizens.[16]

The USA PATRIOT Act, however, made "material support" to *any* of its newly-created categories of "terrorist organizations"—i.e. including to any undesignated group that uses force for any unlawful purpose other than personal enrichment—a basis to deny a person admission to the U.S., to deport a person already here, and to bar him or her from all forms of refugee protection. The burden was on the giver of material support to show that he or she "did not know, and

should not reasonably have known, that [his or her provision of material support] would further the organization's terrorist activity."

The REAL ID Act and the Proliferation of "Terrorism" Bars

"When Congress passed the Real ID Act last year, it presumably did not intend to prevent human rights victims all over the world from entering the United States. Its goal was to keep terrorists and those who support them from resettling in the United States as Refugees. The legislative language, however, was irresponsibly broad; its effects have been cruel to people already oppressed by vile regimes and terrorist groups. The law needs to be changed."

Editorial, "Real Injustice," *Washington Post*, March 18, 2006

Enacted in May 2005, the REAL ID Act wrought an additional and significant expansion of the immigration law's "terrorism"-related provisions.[17] It did this in two ways.

First, the REAL ID Act expanded the immigration law's grounds of inadmissibility related to terrorism, contained in section 212(a)(3)(B) of the Immigration & Nationality Act. The grounds of inadmissibility in the immigration law bar the entry of a person to the United States, and prevent a person already here from being granted permanent residence. The new law made ineligible for entry or permanent residence, for example, anyone who "endorses or espouses" terrorist activity; anyone who has received "military-type training" from a terrorist organization; anyone who is a member of a terrorist organization (regardless of whether the group is a Tier I or Tier II organization, or an undesignated Tier III group). The REAL ID Act even made a person inadmissible simply for being the spouse or child of a person deemed inadmissible under these provisions. The REAL ID Act broadened the USA PATRIOT Act's definition of a "Tier III terrorist organization" to include any group that has a subgroup that engages in "terrorist activity." It also altered the bar relating to "material support" to a "Tier III" group, so that a person who knowingly provided "material support" to a "Tier III terrorist organization" could now escape liability only if she could show by clear and convincing evidence that she did not know and should not reasonably have known that the group "was a terrorist organization."

Second, the REAL ID Act amended section 237(a)(4)(B) of the immigration law (which previously made "engaging in terrorist activity" grounds for deportation) to provide that anyone described in any of the newly expanded grounds of inadmissibility related to "terrorism" was now also deportable. The immigration law's grounds of deportability, as the term suggests, allow the deportation of a person already in the United States, even one who entered the country legally and/or has been granted permanent status here. Historically,

the grounds that will allow a person to be barred from admission to the United States have been broader than the grounds that will allow the deportation of a person already here. As far as the law's "terrorism"-related provisions were concerned, the REAL ID Act changed that, and made the "terrorism"-related grounds of deportability coextensive with the inadmissibility grounds. The bars to asylum and withholding of removal relating to "terrorist activity" both refer to the deportability ground at section 237(a)(4)(B), so with the passage of the REAL ID Act, anyone described in *any* of the new long list of inadmissibility grounds at section 212(a)(3)(B) is now barred from all forms of refugee protection.

4. The Crisis—Reinterpretation of "Terrorist Activity" and Extreme Interpretation of Everything Else

"The problem begins with a sloppy definition of terrorism written into a 1990 immigration law. It was compounded after the 9/11 terrorist attacks by the Bush administration's overly aggressive and rigid interpretations of what constitutes material support for terrorism."

Editorial, "Terrorism's Victims," *New York Times*, March 9, 2007

SOON AFTER THE PASSAGE of the USA PATRIOT Act in 2001, questions arose within the then-Immigration & Naturalization Service, particularly those offices dealing with refugees and asylum seekers, as to how the USA PATRIOT Act amendments should be interpreted. What exactly was "material support"? What kind of support counted, and how much support was required to trigger the bar? What about people who were forced to give to armed groups under duress? Pending legal guidance on all these questions, the Asylum Office began placing on "hold" asylum applicants who reported any number of different kinds of interaction—voluntary or involuntary—with a number of armed groups. Asylum applicants from Colombia, for example, who had been forced to provide goods or services to guerrilla or paramilitary groups, found themselves in bureaucratic limbo. From the applicants' perspective, their requests for asylum disappeared into a black hole. The only information most of them could obtain from the Asylum Office was that their cases were pending, or "required further review."

> Mariana, a nurse in Colombia, came from a family of active supporters of the Colombian government. Her family had brought her up to value public service. She worked for the Ministry of Health, and in her spare time, volunteered in poor communities in her city. While doing this volunteer work, Mariana was kidnapped by members of the *Fuerzas Armadas Revolucionarias de Colombia* (FARC). The guerrillas abducted Mariana and took her to a FARC member who had been shot, forcing her at gunpoint to treat him. Before returning her to her home, the guerrillas threatened her life and the lives of her family if she notified the authorities. The FARC abducted her several more times after that, for the same purpose. They made

it clear to her that they were watching her every move. Terrified that they would kill her and her family if she did not cooperate, and seeing no escape from them in Colombia, she fled to the United States with her young daughter. She applied for asylum and in her application described what had happened to her. After her interview at the Asylum Office, Mariana received no decision. She made repeated inquiries about the status of her case, to no avail. Years passed. Her life and her daughter's life seemed to be suspended.

Then, in the summer of 2006, DHS abruptly rejected her application for asylum, stating: "There are reasonable grounds for regarding you as a danger to the security of the United States in that you have provided material support to those who engage in terrorist activity." DHS initiated proceedings before the immigration court to deport Mariana and her daughter to Colombia. After her case was brought to the attention of a Senate subcommittee, Mariana was asked to testify at a congressional hearing on the impact the "terrorism bars" were having on refugees like her and her daughter. "I have been caught for 7 years," she explained to the Senate subcommittee. "I don't know what to do at this moment. That is why I am here. I decided to come . . . to speak for me and speak up for the other people that are in the same situation."[18]

During the period from 2001 to early 2005, however, people applying for asylum in immigration court proceedings, as opposed to before the Asylum Office, often encountered a somewhat different approach. Trial attorneys representing the Immigration & Naturalization Service (after 2003 the Department of Homeland Security's bureau of Immigration & Customs Enforcement (ICE)) in immigration court in many cases still took the position that duress was indeed a defense to the "material support" bar; they did this either explicitly or by never seeking to apply the bar to people who had given to armed groups under coercion. A number of Immigration Judges were of the same view.[19] As for the definition of "terrorist activity" and "terrorist organization" itself, the immigration courts and the government attorneys litigating cases in that forum on INS/DHS's behalf continued for the most part to apply those definitions with some degree of discernment, and either never thought of invoking them, or rejected this option, in cases where doing so would have produced outcomes that were absurd or contrary to long-standing precedents established under earlier versions of the statute.

But in late 2004 and early 2005, the agencies in charge of enforcing the "terrorism bars" began to interpret the "terrorist activity" definition to nearly the fullest extent of its over-breadth and to interpret the other terrorism-related provisions of the immigration law in increasingly extreme ways. Lawyers representing the Departments of Justice and Homeland Security in immigration cases before the federal courts and the immigration courts now enforced a uniform position that the "material support" bar applied to anyone who had given anything to a "terrorist organization," regardless of whether the person gave of his own free will or at the point of a gun.[20] Attorneys working for the Department of Homeland Security began to take this line across the board, including in cases before the immigration courts and the Board of Immigration Appeals.

At the same time, the Departments of Homeland Security, Justice, and State all began to define as a "terrorist activity" for immigration purposes virtually any use of armed force by a non-state actor (apolitical armed robbers excepted). The immigration law, as noted earlier, defines as "terrorist activity" any use of a weapon with intent to endanger the safety of one or more individuals or to cause substantial damage to property, "which is *unlawful* under the laws of the place where it is committed (or which, if it had been committed in the United States, would be *unlawful* under the laws of the United States or any State)" (emphasis added). Human Rights First believes that the use of the term "unlawful" should allow this definition to be read, consistently with U.S. obligations under the Refugee Convention, not to

apply to uses of force in internal or international armed conflicts, for example, that do not violate the 1949 Geneva Conventions. Nearly every state in the world has agreed to be bound by these international legal obligations, many of whose provisions are now accepted as customary international law. These provisions of international humanitarian law should thus be considered part of "the laws of the place" where such conflicts occur. This is not the way the "terrorist activity" definition is currently being read by any of the federal agencies involved in enforcing it, however, and their position has been upheld by the Board of Immigration Appeals and, more recently, the U.S. Court of Appeals for the Ninth Circuit.[21]

Since the statutory definition of a "Tier III terrorist organization" was built on that definition of "terrorist activity," the Department of Homeland Security also began defining as a "terrorist organization" any collection of human beings who had taken up arms (or included a "subgroup" that had done so) in any situation other than service in their national armies, and for any purpose other than personal enrichment.[22]

In addition, the Department of Homeland Security, in particular, began to read other provisions of the law in an increasingly expansive way, by:

- applying the "Tier III" definition retroactively to groups that had given up violence or ceased to exist altogether;

- classifying groups as "Tier III" groups based on the actions of their coalition partners;

- treating victims of armed groups as supporters of the very groups that extorted goods or services from them under threat of violence;

- applying the "terrorism bars" to the acts of children as if they were adults;

- treating minimal contributions as "material support;"

- interpreting "material support" to cover virtually anything (including non-violent speech and other lawful political activity—e.g. writing for a student newspaper or distributing political flyers) that a person did in connection with his or her association with a group deemed to be a "terrorist organization;" and

- redefining medical care as "material support."

Another of the immigration law's "terrorism"-related provisions, which bars a person from entry, permanent residence, and refugee protection simply for being the spouse or child of a person deemed to fall within the scope of any of the immigration law's "terrorism"-related provisions, has extended the effects of these laws and interpretations to the immediate families of those affected.

Redefining Victims of Repressive Regimes as Terrorists: The "Tier III" Embarrassment

"Shockingly, under today's laws, Jews who bravely resisted and survived Nazi terror would be excluded from refuge in the United States. Under current policy, the Warsaw ghetto uprising would be considered a 'terrorist activity' because it involved the use of weapons against persons or property for reasons other than 'mere personal monetary gain.'"

Letter to President Bush from leaders of the American Jewish Community (July 21, 2006) [23]

The Department of Homeland Security's new interpretation of the "terrorist organization" definition first became clear in early 2005, after several ethnic Chin refugees fleeing political, religious, and ethnic persecution in Burma presented themselves at the U.S. border in El Paso, Texas, and asked for asylum. Burma's ethnic minority groups, many of whom are also religious minorities, have suffered particularly harsh treatment under the military regimes that have ruled the country since overthrowing the democratically elected government there in 1962. The U.S. Secretary of State has designated Burma as a "country of particular concern" under the International Religious Freedom Act for particularly severe violations of religious freedom every year since 1999. The Chin refugees who arrived in El Paso in the summer of 2004 reported having suffered abuses in Burma that included arbitrary arrest, torture, prolonged detention at forced labor, and suppression of their Christian religion. [24]

These asylum seekers, several of whom had previously been involved in the peaceful pro-democracy movement that was brutally suppressed in Burma in the late 1980's, reported to U.S. immigration authorities that they had provided varying forms of assistance to the Chin National Front (CNF), a Chin political movement that includes an armed wing, the Chin National Army. On this basis, the Department of Homeland Security argued that all of them were barred from protection in the United States for having provided "material support to a terrorist organization." [25]

A refugee's participation in, or assistance to, an armed rebellion, even against a regime that does not allow political change through the ballot box, is certainly relevant to his possible exclusion from protection under the Refugee Convention. But the proper focus under the Convention is whether the refugee's involvement was such as to make him responsible for excludable acts—war crimes, crimes against humanity, or serious non-political crimes, including acts of terrorism. Under the government's earlier understanding of the statute, and for years before the enactment of the USA PATRIOT Act, immigration judges and asylum officers evaluating asylum claims had considered the applicant's actual acts, as well as the acts of the group which she helped further, in determining whether she should be excluded from protection under the provision of the immigration law that bars from refugee protection anyone who "ordered, incited, assisted, or otherwise participated in" the persecution of others. [26] Involvement with armed groups engaged in hostilities against the United States could also trigger the separate statutory bar excluding from protection anyone whom "there are reasonable grounds for regarding . . . as a danger to the security of the United States." [27]

In the case of these Burmese Chin refugees, the Immigration Judge ultimately agreed with DHS's argument that they must be denied asylum and withholding of removal under the "terrorism bars" based on the support they had provided to the CNF. This decision was not based on any finding that the CNF, or these individual applicants, had committed war crimes or otherwise violated the laws of armed conflict, or that they posed any sort of danger to the United States. The Immigration Judge found only that the CNF's armed wing was engaged in military operations against the Burmese army, and that the applicants were aware of this fact.[28] On appeal, the BIA upheld the Immigration Judge's conclusions, in a decision that was published under the name *Matter of S-K-*, after the initials of the asylum seeker whose case it decided first.[29]

The result of the BIA's holding in *Matter of S-K-* was to allow a refugee to be excluded from protection for contributing to any group that included an armed wing, without any showing that the group—much less the refugee herself—was responsible for conduct that would justify a person's exclusion from refugee protection. Rather, the simple fact that a group had used armed force, against anyone, whatever the circumstances and possible justifications, was enough to exclude all of its members and anyone who provided the group with "material support."

> "We are finding that a Christian member of the ethnic Chin minority in Burma, who clearly has a well-founded fear of being persecuted by one of the more repressive governments in the world, one that the United States Government views as illegitimate, is ineligible to avail herself of asylum in the United States despite posing no threat to the security of this country. . . [I]t is difficult to conclude that this is what Congress intended."
>
> Board Member Juan P. Osuna, concurring in
> *Matter of S-K-*, 23 I.&.N. 936 (BIA 2006)

While Congress in late 2007 passed legislation removing the Chin National Front and nine other named groups from the immigration law's definition of a "Tier III terrorist organization," the "Tier III" definition continues to be applied to a growing number of groups that had not been characterized in this way in the past. These groups include:

- All Iraqis, and Iraqi groups, who rose up against Saddam Hussein in the 1990's, including those who took part in the failed uprising at the end of the 1991 Gulf War that was encouraged by the first President Bush;

- All Iraqis, and Iraqi groups, that later fought against Saddam Hussein's armies in conjunction with the Coalition forces that ultimately overthrew his regime in 2003;

- All of the Afghan *mujahidin* groups that fought the Soviet invasion in the 1980's, with U.S. support;

- The Democratic Unionist Party and the Ummah Party, two of the largest democratic opposition parties in Sudan, many of whose members were forced to flee the country in the years after the 1989 military coup that brought current President Omar Al-Bashir to power;

- The Sudan People's Liberation Movement/Army (SPLM/SPLA), the South Sudanese armed opposition movement that after years of civil war in pursuit of southern self-determination is now the ruling party of an autonomous Government of South Sudan;

- Various groups that fought in Central America in the 1980's, and have either ceased to exist or only exist as political parties and are active players in the political process in the countries in question;

- Virtually all Ethiopian and Eritrean political parties and movements, past and present;

- The Awami League, one of the main political parties in Bangladesh;

- Every group ever to have fought the ruling military junta in Burma that was not included in the legislation that removed the Chin National Front and others from the scope of the Tier III definition;

- Any group that has used armed force against the regime in Iran since the 1979 revolution;

- The Movement for Democratic Change (MDC), the main political opposition to President Robert Mugabe of Zimbabwe.

The result of the description of all of these groups as "Tier III" terrorist organizations is that asylum seekers or refugees who gave to, fought with, or had or have a range of other associations with these groups are now being labeled as members or supporters of "terrorist organizations" and seeing their claims denied or placed on indefinite hold.

The number of groups being characterized as "undesignated terrorist organizations" is growing daily, invisible to the public eye. Human Rights First receives regular inquiries from immigration lawyers and refugee advocates as to whether a particular organization "is a Tier III group." The problem with the Tier III definition is that there is no answer to that question. A group "is a Tier III group" when some immigration adjudicator, somewhere, says that it is. And when that happens, there is no public announcement. (A federal judge recently ordered DHS to file "the list" of groups USCIS was considering to be "Tier III terrorist organizations." DHS filed its response under seal, so that it is not publicly available. As far as Human Rights First is aware, there is no central official "list" of groups deemed to be "Tier III" organizations.[30])

Adding to the uncertainty of the situation is the Department of Homeland Security's practice of treating any act of violence by any number of members of a group as a basis for deeming the group to "engage in" terrorist activity. The statutory definition of a Tier III group is certainly extremely broad, but this is one example of the many ways in which its reach has been broadened by the way immigration agencies have chosen to interpret it. Even the text of the present statute should require some examination of the scope of whatever violence is being attributed to a group and of the extent to which such violence is authorized by the group's leadership, before a conclusion is made that the group or a subgroup thereof "engages in terrorist activity."[31] The process by which groups that *do* appear on the State Department's lists of terrorist organizations come to be designated or listed as Tier I or Tier II groups does allow for consideration of those factors. And the acts that trigger Tier I and Tier II designations, in practice if not as a matter of legal definition, have generally involved significant levels of violence targeted against civilians or non-combatants.

Retroactive Application of the Tier III Definition to Groups That Have Given Up Violence or No Longer Exist

"It is frankly a rather embarrassing matter that I still have to waive in my own counterpart, the foreign minister of South Africa, not to mention the great leader Nelson Mandela."

Secretary of State Condoleezza Rice (April 2008)

The USA PATRIOT Act defined a Tier III "terrorist organization" as a group that *"engages in"* terrorist activity as defined by the immigration law. This definition was expanded by the REAL ID Act in 2005 to include any group that *"engages in or has a subgroup that engages in"* such activity. The provision of law making members of "terrorist organizations" inadmissible is likewise phrased in the present tense, to bar anyone who "is a member" of such an organization. While the Department of Homeland Security, the Department of State, and the Department of Justice all agree that the membership bar applies only to present members, all three agencies in adjudicating or litigating individual cases are reading the "Tier III" definition in the past tense, to apply to any group that at has at any point used armed force.[32]

This reading of the "Tier III" definition has led the Department of Homeland Security to block the application for permanent residence of an Afghan asylee because as a child he assisted a group that was allied with the United States in opposing the Soviet occupation of his country.

> Jamshid was a young child in 1979 when his family's life in Afghanistan was shattered by the Soviet invasion. Two of his brothers joined the rebellion against the new regime. His father, who had been a member of parliament under a former government, was jailed and tortured by the secret police of the new Soviet-backed regime. In 1983, the valley where the family lived came under continuous bombardment by Soviet and Afghan government troops. Jamshid and his family joined the hundreds of thousands of Afghans who fled to Pakistan as refugees. In Pakistan, Jamshid attended high school, and also took English classes at the American Cultural Center. He also carried supplies for the National Islamic Front of Afghanistan (NIFA), acting at the behest of his older brothers who were then fighting with

the group within Afghanistan. Fearing for his safety, his family sent Jamshid to the United States in 1988. He arrived in this country as an unaccompanied minor at the age of 16, and applied for asylum the following year. Due to extreme administrative delays, he was finally granted asylum in 1998. In 1999, he applied for permanent residence.

In February 2008, Jamshid's application for permanent residence was denied. The denial letter (reproduced in redacted form as Appendix C to this report) states: "In your asylum application you provided a statement that you have actively supported the Mujahidin since 1984 when you were twelve years old. You state that you helped carry supplies such as weapons, ammunition, flour, and sugar from Pakistan to Afghanistan to the soldiers fighting there." Jamshid was 17 years old when he made that statement in his request for asylum. The denial letter states that the Mujahidin "meets the current definition of an undesignated terrorist organization."

The particular group that Jamshid had helped, the NIFA, was generally viewed as the most moderate of the numerous groups that fought politically and militarily against the Soviet occupation of Afghanistan. Its ideology was nationalist and royalist; its leader, Pir Sayed Ahmad Gailani, was an in-law of the royal family whose own prestige derived from his role as the head of the Qadiriya Sufi order, which represented a liberal tendency in Afghan Islam. The United States itself provided support to the NIFA and other Afghan *mujahidin* groups in the 1980's.[33]

By the time the "Tier III" definition was first enacted in 2001, the NIFA had effectively ceased to exist even as a political entity and was no longer functioning as a military force. Its former leaders had assumed an active political role in exile during the last years of Taliban rule, and went on to assume high positions in government and Afghan civil society under current President Hamid Karzai. Two years before Jamshid's application for permanent residence was denied, a former NIFA leader, now member of the upper house of the Afghan National Assembly, was a guest of First Lady Laura Bush at the 2006 State of the Union Address.[34] Jamshid, meanwhile, has no idea when he may finally become a permanent resident of the country he has called home for over 20 years. His application, reopened in the spring of 2008, remains on hold.

As noted earlier, terrorism-related bars to entry or to immigration status are justified to protect the security of the United States and to penalize those guilty of criminal

wrongdoing. Neither of these purposes is served by retroactively defining as Tier III "terrorist organizations" an ever-growing list of groups that no longer exist, or have long since joined the regular political process and now exist only as purely political entities.[35] A person who poses a threat to the security of the United States, or who has himself engaged in "terrorist activity," or who is coming to the United States in order to do so, is already barred from admission to the United States under separate provisions of the Immigration & Nationality Act. Anyone who has committed a serious non-political crime abroad or who has persecuted others is also barred from refugee protection.[36] What security purpose is served by excluding—or denying refugee protection to—a person who does *not* pose a threat to this country and is not subject to any of the immigration law's long list of other bars, simply because he made a contribution long ago to a group that no longer exists or is now an established political party?

One result of this reading of the statute was to treat the African National Congress (ANC) as a "Tier III terrorist organization" under the 2001 USA PATRIOT Act definition, based on its actions in South Africa under apartheid. While some ANC members from that period might be independently inadmissible to the United States based on their own acts, characterizing the ANC generally as a "Tier III" group meant that ANC members who had been active in the party during that era—many of them now senior leaders of the post-apartheid South African government—were barred from the United States based on their membership alone. In April 2008, urging Congressional action to correct this, Secretary of State Condoleezza Rice testified to a Senate committee: "It is frankly a rather embarrassing matter that I still have to waive in my own counterpart, the foreign minister of South Africa, not to mention the great leader Nelson Mandela."[37] In 2007, South Africa's former ambassador to the United States, Barbara Masekela, had been unable to receive a waiver in time to visit a sick cousin in the United States, who later died. It took special legislation, signed into law on July 2, 2008, to remove the ANC from the scope of the immigration law's "Tier III" definition.[38]

The ANC, however, is only one of many groups that have been defined as "Tier III terrorist organizations" as they are undergoing—or after having undergone—a transition to non-violent political participation. Many refugees from Southern Sudan, for example, are currently deemed to be barred from permanent residence based on their past support to, or present membership in, the Sudan People's Liberation Movement (SPLM). The SPLM is the political wing of the Sudan People's Liberation Army (SPLA), which waged civil war against successive central governments in Khartoum from 1983 to 2005, when it entered into a Comprehensive Peace Accord with the Sudanese government. Under this agreement, the SPLM joined the government, and its leader, John Garang, became Vice-President of Sudan. In January 2006, John Garang's widow was a guest of First Lady Laura Bush at the State of the Union address to the U.S. Congress. On the occasion of the inauguration of new SPLA headquarters in 2008, the U.S. Department of State announced that the United States was "privileged to partner with the SPLA in transforming it into a professional military force."[39] U.S. support for the SPLA continues under the present administration: the U.S. State Department recently noted that "U.S. assistance is being used to assist the GoSS [Government of South Sudan] and the GoSS's Sudan People's Liberation Army (SPLA) with security sector reform, including infrastructure, command headquarters, and transportation projects."[40]

Yet at the same time that the United States government has itself been providing technical and material assistance to the SPLA, it continues to refuse permanent residence to SPLM/SPLA leaders and supporters who fled to the United States during the civil war period. In February 2008, for example, the Department of Homeland Security denied the application for permanent residence of a Sudanese refugee, Kun Garbang, stating: "Due to your being a current member and representative of SPLM . . . you are inadmissible." Kun Garbang and his family had been living in the United States since 2001. Two of his sons had joined the Marines with his blessing. At the time when Mr. Garbang received this letter, one son had been serving in Iraq for more than two years.[41]

Terrorism As Contagious Disease: Misunderstanding the Notion of "Subgroup"

The statutory definition of a Tier III "terrorist organization" covers any "group of two or more individuals, whether organized or not, which engages in, or has a subgroup which engages in" activities defined as "terrorist" under the immigration law. In a number of decisions involving applications for permanent residence by people previously granted asylum or refugee status, the Department of Homeland Security has used this language to characterize groups as Tier III "terrorist organizations" based not on their own actions but on those of their coalition partners. This was DHS's basis for blocking the path to permanent residence for Salih, a democratic activist from Sudan granted asylum in the United States 12 years ago:

> Salih was a member of the democratic opposition in Sudan after the 1989 coup that brought current president Omar Al-Bashir to power. When that coup was followed by a major crackdown on all forms of peaceful political opposition activity, Salih fled to the United States in 1993 and was granted asylum in 1997. He subsequently applied for permanent residence. In early 2008, U.S. Citizenship & Immigration Services denied that application on the grounds that Salih's membership in the Democratic Unionist Party (DUP) and in the National Democratic Alliance, a coalition of nearly all Sudanese opposition groups to which the DUP belongs, made him a "member of a terrorist organization." Salih's application was later reopened, but remains on hold.[42] The DUP is one of the two largest and oldest political parties in Sudan—the other being the Ummah Party, which the Department of Homeland Security is also treating as "Tier III" group. These two parties were partners in the democratically elected coalition government overthrown by the 1989 military coup, and have been in opposition since that time. At the time of that 1989 coup, the leader of the DUP had negotiated a ceasefire agreement with the southern Sudan People's Liberation Movement, in an attempt to end the long-running civil war between the predominantly Muslim North and the South of Sudan whose inhabitants are largely Christian and animist.

The denial letter Salih received quotes from Salih's application for asylum, approved over 10 years earlier, which described the activities that allegedly make him a member of a "terrorist organization": "In your asylum claim, you state that you formally joined the DUP when you entered Ain Shams University. In 1992 you participated in a conference organized by the Fund for Peace for the DUP. You further claimed to have been very active within the activities of the DUP." All of these activities took place in the late 1980's and early 1990's. To explain its denial of permanent residence to Salih, USCIS quotes from a variety of internet sources—all referring to periods of time after Salih's arrival in the United States—that describe how the Sudan People's Liberation Army (SPLA), the South Sudanese rebel group, in the mid-1990's joined the National Democratic Alliance, the opposition umbrella coalition of which the DUP was already a leading member. According to the USCIS denial letter, the SPLA's having joined the National Democratic Alliance over 10 years ago means that "the DUP and other members of the NDA meet the current definition of an undesignated terrorist organization."

This denial letter—like many of the others Human Rights First has seen that were issued to present and former members of the Sudanese democratic opposition—is remarkable for its lack of attention to chronology. Not only was Salih already in the United States by the time the SPLA joined the DUP as part of the National Democratic Alliance, by the time his application for permanent residence was denied, the SPLA itself had laid down its arms, as noted earlier.

USCIS's characterization of the DUP as a Tier III "terrorist organization" appeared to rest not so much on the DUP's own actions but on the fact that it considers the *SPLA* to be a Tier III "terrorist organization."[43] The SPLA and the DUP were both members of the National Democratic Alliance, the logic goes, therefore the SPLA should be considered a "subgroup" of the DUP. While the term "subgroup" is not defined by the statute, to consider one group a subgroup of another because the two groups are part of a broader coalition misunderstands the realities of political life and has disturbing implications for politics and peace-making in countries like Sudan. The DUP and the SPLA are, and always have been, very different organizations: they have entirely separate leadership, their members are drawn from different ethnic, regional, and

religious groups within Sudanese society, and they have distinct political agendas.

Similar reasoning appears in a number of letters Human Rights First has seen that were issued by USCIS to asylees from Ethiopia who had been affiliated with political parties that appear to have been characterized as "Tier III" groups based on their association with *other* political parties.[44]

By USCIS's logic, Human Rights First would be considered a "subgroup" of the U.S. Conference of Catholic Bishops, because both groups are members of Refugee Council U.S.A., a coalition of U.S. non-governmental organizations focused on refugee protection. While it is certainly true that the two groups have joined together in coalition to further specific shared goals, as both state and non-state groups typically do, this does not mean that Human Rights First takes direction from the Vatican (or vice versa), nor are individuals who make donations to Human Rights First contributing to the Catholic Church. To the extent the immigration law continues to make association with "Tier III" organizations a basis for denial of status and refugee protection in the United States, it is critical that these judgments be made based on an assessment of the group with which the applicant was actually associated, and of the time period during which he or she was associated with it.

Redefining Victims of Terrorist Organizations as Terrorists

"But it was for my child, don't they understand that it was to ransom my child?"

> Refugee's reaction to government's position that payments to armed groups made under duress constitute "material support" to terrorism

"I do not think that there is one out of any 535 of us who voted on this legislation [the USA PATRIOT Act]—whether for it or against it—who would ever have contemplated that somebody who paid ransom to get back a loved one who was kidnapped would be materially supporting terrorists or terrorism. That clearly could not be the intent of anybody let alone the entire Congress in this legislation, and if somebody at Homeland Security or any other agency is saying that that is the intent of Congress . . . then I do not know that there is any justice here."

Rep. Gary Ackerman (March 26, 2007)[45]

At the same time that it was expanding its reading of the "terrorist organization" definition to cover groups like the Chin National Front, the Department of Homeland Security also applied the "material support" bar to unwilling victims of armed groups, as did the Department of Justice in litigating asylum cases before the federal courts. Both agencies have taken the position that the "terrorism bars" are not susceptible to any interpretive limitations, exceptions, or defenses unless these are explicitly spelled out in the statute.[46] One early and glaring example of this legal position in action came when the State Department in 2005 attempted to resettle in the United States a number of refugee women who had suffered terrible harm at the hands of West African rebel groups. One Liberian woman had been gang-raped and held hostage by rebels who also forced her to cook and clean for them. As this woman was on the brink of beginning a new life in the United States, the Department of Homeland Security (whose officers must approve all applicants for refugee resettlement before they can be brought to the United States) placed her application on hold, on the theory that the cooking and cleaning this woman had been forced to do constituted "material support" to her captors and rapists.[47]

The same reasoning led the application for permanent residence of an elderly asylee from Afghanistan to disappear into an administrative black hole:

> An officer in the Afghan armed forces from the 1950's to 1978, Ziad was jailed and tortured in the late 1970's for his opposition to the Soviet occupation of his country. Determined not to abandon their country, Ziad and his wife Fahima, a teacher, survived the Soviet-backed regimes in Afghanistan, and labored under suspicion through the period of *Mujahidin* control from 1992 to 1996. Then came the Taliban. Confined to their home because Fahima was not willing to comply with the Taliban's severe restrictions on women appearing in public and because Ziad was afraid the Taliban would target him for political reasons, the couple, together with a few other teachers, decided secretly to open a girls' school in their house. The school had been in operation for about a year when the Taliban raided the house and found a few students, two teachers, Ziad, Fahima, their daughter, and evidence of ongoing teaching in the form of books, notebooks, and teaching supplies. They also found photos of Ziad in military uniform taken while he was studying in the United States in the 1970's. The Taliban accused Ziad and Fahima not only of operating a girls' school in violation of their edicts, but also of being agents of the United States. Ziad, Fahima, and their daughter were all beaten severely and repeatedly interrogated in a jail where Fahima and her daughter could hear the screams of other prisoners being tortured. Ziad was told he was going to be executed.
>
> After the family had spent several weeks under these conditions, a corrupt Taliban official offered to release them secretly in exchange for a $5,000 bribe. Ziad had nothing like that amount of money, but the Taliban official ultimately agreed to take jewelry, carpets, antiques, and other personal possessions that the family had at home. After their release, Ziad, Fahima, and their daughter fled to the United States, where they applied for asylum. In his application, Ziad related in detail the facts summarized above. Their application was granted. In 2002, Ziad applied for permanent residence. Caught in backlog after backlog, his application languished for over six years. In 2008, Ziad was informed that his application was now on hold because the carpets, jewelry, and household goods he had allowed the corrupt official to take in order to save his family's life were being construed as "material support" to the Taliban.[48] Ziad, now an elderly man, eventually received his permanent residence in February 2009—nearly two years after DHS implemented waivers with respect to people forced to give to undesignated armed groups—but only after he lost his federal medical coverage for a period of time due to the excessive delays in processing his application for permanent residence, and suffered a stroke.

DHS has now implemented its discretionary authority to grant waivers of the "material support" bar—and only the "material support" bar—in cases of coercion. DHS has granted 2,810 waivers of this type to date in connection with initial applications for asylum or refugee resettlement. 2,556 of these applications have been to refugees seeking resettlement from overseas, 253 to asylum seekers here in the United States. DHS has also granted waivers in connection with 1,821 applications for permanent residence or family reunification filed by asylees and refugees previously granted protection in the United States, a large proportion of which were duress cases.[49] While DHS's implementation of this waiver authority offers the prospect of relief for asylum seekers and refugees whose applications are pending before DHS, it means that even these applicants remain subject to double adjudication (first on the merits of their application and then on whether they should be granted a duress waiver), according to a process laid out in a May 24, 2007 USCIS memorandum.[50]

In applications pending before the Department of Homeland Security, the ensuing delays can be significant. One asylum seeker represented *pro bono* through Human Rights First, a refugee from Bhutan whose case was profiled in our August 2006 report on this same topic, finally received a grant of asylum in September 2009—three and a half years after his asylum interview, and nearly nine months after DHS Secretary Michael Chertoff authorized waivers to be granted to victims of Tier II groups like the Nepalese Maoists (the category into which DHS probably believed this man's case fell). This is in contrast to the Asylum Office's standard practice of issuing decisions to most affirmative asylum applicants two weeks after their asylum office interviews. A significant part of the delay in this and other asylum cases Human Rights First has monitored that have required "waivers" resulted from delays— of months, in some cases—in forwarding the applicant's file from the local office that interviewed the applicant to the Headquarters office that was to review it for waiver adjudication, and then back to the local office for issuance of a decision.

For asylum seekers whose cases are pending before the immigration court, DHS's waiver process is not working, as is described in greater detail below in Part 6 of this report. Applicants whose only crime was to be crime victims continue to suffer prolonged detention, unnecessary separation from loved ones stranded in war zones, and years of uncertainty about their fates, as a result of the government's decision to characterize the harm they suffered as a ground for excluding them from the refugee protection to which they are otherwise entitled.

Estimating the number of asylum seekers in this situation is difficult, because the Department of Justice does not track the reasons why immigration judges and the Board of Immigration Appeals deny asylum to applicants. DHS Immigration and Customs Enforcement (ICE) does not release information on the number of cases it litigates before the immigration courts where it invokes the "terrorism"-related provisions of the immigration law as bars to asylum or other relief from deportation. U.S. Citizenship & Immigration Services, which of all agencies involved in this process has been the most conscientious both about keeping statistics and sharing that information with non-governmental organizations working on these issues, is only able to track cases that are pending before its own offices. For reasons described in Part 6 below, cases in immigration court proceedings are not referred to USCIS until an administratively final order of removal is issued (i.e. until the applicant is ordered deported from the United States by the immigration judge and does not appeal, or is ordered deported by the Board of Immigration Appeals), and this referral process has happened only in a handful of cases to date.

It is not clear what purpose is served by DHS's decision to treat victims of coercion at the hands of armed groups as supporters of those who victimized them. In these cases, the applicants were the ones who told the U.S. government the facts the DHS invokes to bar them from protection. Many of them fled to the United States in order to escape from the rebel groups that had extorted goods and services from them, and to ensure that they would never be subject to such coercion again.

No Place for Children: The Application of the Terrorism Bars to Minors

In addition to redefining adult victims of coercion as supporters of terrorism, DHS has also applied a range of the immigration law's "terrorism bars" to children, or to applicants who are now adults but were children at the time of the events at issue.

> Martine was 12 years old when armed rebels abducted her from her family's home in the eastern part of the Democratic Republic of the Congo.[51] She remained a captive of the rebels for approximately three years. She witnessed the death and injury of other child soldiers, and lived in fear of the abuses that she and the other children there suffered on a daily basis. The rebels forced the children to smoke marijuana to dull their terror before sending them into battle. Girls like Martine were also made to perform domestic labor and were subject to constant rape by commanders and other soldiers. After she was finally released from the rebel army, Martine began working as a counselor for other demobilized girls, who were particularly stigmatized in their communities because of the sexual abuse they were assumed to have suffered. Working with the local NGO that had negotiated her own demobilization, Martine traveled to the United States and to Europe to speak out about the particular plight of girl soldiers and to press for prosecution of rebel commanders for the sexual abuse committed against them. As word of her activities in the United States got back to the Congo, it became too dangerous for Martine to return home, and she was forced to apply for asylum here. Martine's application has been placed on indefinite hold because she is a former child soldier.

Although DHS has implemented "waivers" for asylum applicants who provided "material support" to rebel groups under duress, it has failed to make similar provision for those who were forced to take part in combat, or forced to receive "military-type" training from an armed group. Still a teenager, Martine has adapted well to life in the United States, learning English and contributing to her local community. She will be graduating from high school next year. But without any legal status, she has no security in the new life she is building here, and no way of paying for college.

U.S. and international law have long recognized the diminished responsibility of children, and the Department of Homeland Security has not articulated a security rationale for its refusal to acknowledge the legal relevance of childhood to the application of the "terrorism bars" in children's asylum cases.[52] These young people are here in the United States because they "voted with their feet" against the wars in which they were made to fight—or to carry loads, or to wash laundry, or to be sex slaves to their commanders.

> Lino Nakwa, a native of South Sudan, was a child of 12 when soldiers from the Sudan People's Liberation Army (SPLA) abducted him and his older brother. The two boys were taken to an SPLA training camp where they were given minimal training and were made to work for the rebels. They were held there for a month, until they were able to escape. Lino made his way to Kenya. After years as a refugee in East Africa, Lino was eventually resettled in Kentucky, arriving in the United States in 2003 at the age of 24. In the United States, Lino worked multiple jobs to put himself through community college, and went on to study for a bachelor's degree. In February 2008, he was a business finance major and on the dean's list at his university, when he received a letter in the mail informing him that he was inadmissible to the United States as one who had received "military-type training" from a "terrorist organization."[53]

> "Information in your file," the denial letter stated, "reveals that you and your brother were forced to attend a SPLA training camp for approximately one month." This "information" came from Lino himself, who had described his abduction and his month in the SPLA training camp when he had applied for refugee resettlement. "It was the reason I fled my country," he explained to a reporter. "It was the reason I came here, and now that same information is being used to take me back." Lino's college classmates and many friends and supporters in the Lexington community publicly protested what was happening to him, and his representatives in Congress wrote to DHS on his behalf. In April 2008, his case was reopened, only to be put back on hold like so many others denied at the same time. It is still pending. Lino graduated from college in May 2009, but still does not know when he may become a permanent resident of the only secure home he has known since childhood.

While DHS has implemented its waiver authority with respect to the "material support" bar in cases where applicants gave to armed groups under duress, it has not done the same for any of the other "terrorism"-related bars, so that refugees who "received military-type training" from a non-state armed group after being conscripted against their wills, for example, or who were forced to take part in combat, currently are not being considered for waivers.

Four Dollars and Your Lunch: The Distortion of "Material Support"

"When I use a word," Humpty Dumpty said in rather a scornful tone, "it means just what I choose it to mean— neither more nor less."
"The question is," said Alice, "whether you can make words mean so many different things."
"The question is," said Humpty Dumpty, "which is to be master—that's all."

(Lewis Carroll, *Through the Looking Glass*)

The immigration law defines as "terrorist activity" the provision of "material support" for the commission of "terrorist activity," to a person who has committed (or plans to commit) "terrorist activity," or to any one of the three types of groups defined as "terrorist organizations" under the immigration law. The language of the statute provides an illustrative list of what is meant by "material support;" "a safe house, transportation, communications, funds, transfer of funds or other material financial benefit, false documentation or identification, weapons (including chemical, biological, or radiological weapons), explosives, or training." The definition's examples all either bear an inherent connection to unlawful activity or are immediately convertible for use to advance such activity.

There is a dearth of case law interpreting these provisions. The Board of Immigration Appeals has issued no precedential decisions on most of the issues they raise. A panel of the U.S. Court of Appeals for the Third Circuit in 2004 held (over strongly worded dissent) that a person who had provided food and helped set up tents for religious ceremonies attended by members of Sikh militant groups had provided "material support" to those militants.[54] In its administrative

adjudications and in the positions it has taken in litigation, the Department of Homeland Security has taken very extreme positions on what constitutes "material support," reading that term to cover minimal contributions, purely political speech and activity, and activity like the provision of medical care that is inherently lawful.

Treating Minimal Contributions As "Material Support"

In individual cases before the Board of Immigration Appeals and the federal courts, lawyers representing the Department of Homeland Security and the Justice Department have indicated on several occasions that they consider that even the most minimal amount of goods or services—a glass of water, five cents—could constitute "material support."[55] Although those particular examples were offered in response to hypothetical questions posed by courts at oral argument, government attorneys and DHS adjudicators have taken the same position in practice in cases that are nearly as extreme, with serious consequences for the refugees in question. For example, DHS's Immigration & Customs Enforcement recently argued—and an immigration judge agreed—that a bagged lunch and the equivalent of $4 constituted "material support."

Louis, a citizen of Burundi, was detained in successive detention centers and county jails in Virginia for more than 20 months after he arrived in the United States at the end of November 2007 and asked for asylum. In his application, he described how he had been robbed on two occasions by members of the *Forces Nationales de Libération* (FNL) rebel group, who had also been threatening him and pressuring him—unsuccessfully— to contribute to their movement. This Hutu rebel movement had been fighting successive governments in Burundi for years. Louis, himself Hutu, did not want to help them because he disapproved of their violence and their many documented abuses against the civilian population. The first of the incidents of robbery Louis described occurred when the bus in which Louis was riding to work was stopped at an FNL roadblock. FNL members made the driver get out of the vehicle and give them everything his passengers had placed in the back, which included Louis's bagged lunch. Louis testified that he later had another series of much more personal encounters with the FNL in which they demanded that he join them and pay them a substantial sum of money. As he kept putting them off, they threatened him and accused him of supporting their political enemies. In the last of these encounters, an FNL member threatened Louis with a bayonet, grabbed him by the collar of his shirt, and told him he had better come up with the contribution they had demanded. In grabbing Louis's shirt, the rebel saw that he had about 5,000 Burundian francs in his shirt pocket, which the rebel grabbed. Louis, who had a much larger sum in his pants pocket and was anxious that the rebels not find that larger sum, suggested that keep the 5,000 francs to buy themselves some beer. The rebels took the 5,000 and left, after warning him that he still needed to pay them the contribution they required. Louis testified that he believed that the rebels probably did in fact use the 5,000 to buy beer. 5,000 Burundian francs is just over $4 at current exchange rates.

In immigration court, DHS claimed that Louis was ineligible for refugee protection because the $4 and the bagged lunch the FNL had taken from him constituted "material support" to the FNL. The immigration judge agreed, though he found Louis's testimony to be credible and found him eligible for asylum but for the "material support" bar. On appeal, the Board of Immigration Appeals agreed with Louis, noting that he never "committed an act" of material support, as the statute explicitly requires, and that even if he had, $4 and a bagged lunch could not be considered "material." DHS finally released Louis in July 2009 after over 20 months in detention and after the filing of a *habeas* petition.[56]

Unfortunately, because the Board of Immigration Appeals decision in Louis's case was unpublished (meaning that it is not binding on the Department of Homeland Security or in other cases before the Board of Immigration Appeals), DHS adjudicators and trial attorneys in other cases continue to take the position that *de minimis* contributions should be considered "material."

The government's insistence on treating even the most minimal "contribution" as "material support" has practical effects, not only for the applicants affected but for the size of the government's own caseload, because a significant proportion of the cases of which Human Rights First is aware that are being affected by the material support provisions of the immigration law involve extremely small amounts of goods or services.

Solomon, for example, an Ethiopian citizen of Oromo ethnicity, was a member of the Oromo Liberation Front (OLF) in the early 1990's. He joined the OLF because he shared its goals of full representation for the Oromo people and recognition of Oromo rights to certain lands in Ethiopia. He was actively involved in the party during the period 1991-1992, a period during which the OLF was the second-largest party in the transitional national government of Ethiopia. During this period, Solomon raised funds from people in his area for refreshments and entertainment at an experimental election in anticipation of the actual election scheduled for 1992. Solomon estimates that the amount of money he raised, important though it was for this purely political purpose, amounted to no more than $30 in U.S. currency. Although the OLF also had an armed wing during this period, so too did the other main partner in the transitional government at that time, now the ruling party in Ethiopia.

Solomon had no role in the actions of the OLF's armed wing but did not consider its activities to be "terrorist," nor was the OLF defined as a "terrorist organization" under U.S. immigration law at that time. The United States government actively encouraged the formation of the transitional government and the kind of democratic participation Solomon was trying to support. Targeted by a crackdown on OLF members that followed the OLF's withdrawal from the government, Solomon fled to the United States in late 1997 and was granted asylum in 1999. In 2008, his application for permanent residence was denied (and later reopened and put on indefinite hold) on the grounds that he was a member of and had provided "material support" to an "undesignated terrorist organization." The denial letter referred to acts of the OLF beginning two years after Solomon's arrival in the United States.[57]

This treatment of small contributions as "material support" is a recurring issue in cases where the Department of Homeland Security is treating as "Tier III terrorist organizations" groups that are also (and often primarily) political opposition parties, most of whose members contributed to the party in the form of minimal membership dues and other non-financial support and political activity bearing no inherent connection to any acts of violence.

Confusing Sympathy, Political Speech and Activity, and Material Support

Lawyers and adjudicators with the Departments of Homeland Security and Justice have also characterized thoughts, speech, and activity that have nothing to do with terrorism as "material support" to terrorist organizations. The immigration law defines "terrorist activity" as activity that is "unlawful," and describes "material support to a terrorist organization" as a form of "terrorist activity."[58] Yet the immigration agencies are construing as "terrorist activity" actions that are lawful under international law, that would be legal in the United States if they were undertaken here, and that in some cases were even legal (although unlawfully repressed) under the law of the countries where they were carried out.

In one recent case before the immigration court, for example, an asylum seeker affiliated with an independence movement in Angola that the immigration court deemed to be a Tier III group testified that a member of the movement had given him posters which he had posted in the streets. The applicant testified that the posters called for the withdrawal of government forces from his native province; they did not call on people to commit acts of violence, nor did they refer to the group to which he belonged. The applicant had also paid minimal membership dues to the group. The Immigration Judge characterized both the membership dues and the applicant's posting of political views as "material support to a terrorist organization."[59] The Department of Homeland Security in adjudicating applications pending before that agency has likewise characterized as "material support" political speech and writing that in the United States would be protected by constitutional guarantees of freedom of speech, or in other cases has characterized *any* political activity a person engaged in as "material support" if the person took part in such activity in connection with, or while affiliated with, any political movement DHS has deemed a "terrorist organization" under the immigration law's definition.

In other cases, the Department of Homeland Security has deemed speech and the dissemination of political writings to be "material support" without making any inquiry into the content of those writings. A refugee from Burma, for example, was denied permanent residence on the grounds that the summary of the applicant's refugee claim in DHS's files— information provided by him and based on which he was admitted to the U.S. as a refugee—indicated that he had "helped" various Burmese organizations, including the All-Burma Students Democratic Front (ABSDF) by "sending back 'stimulating papers' published in Thailand for a relative of his in Burma to distribute." A student group that took up arms in response to the suppression of the 1988 student movement in Burma, the ABSDF fought the Burmese military regime for several years alongside Burma's ethnic insurgent groups. Its members are also known to have been involved in the distribution of pro-democracy publications.[60] This young man's dissemination of literature was described in the denial letter as "material support" to a terrorist organization. Although a number of other Burmese insurgent groups were removed from the scope of the Tier III definition by Congressional action at the end of 2007, the ABSDF was not, so this refugee's case, reopened in the spring of 2008, remains on hold.[61]

Similarly, DHS denied the application for permanent residence of a refugee from Iran, on the grounds—described by the applicant himself in his application for asylum which had been granted years earlier—that as a member of the Iranian National Resistance Movement (more commonly known as the National Movement of Iranian Resistance or NAMIR), he "had publishing equipment and . . . printed and passed out pro-Shah propaganda." The applicant stated that he had been a member of the movement from approximately 1980 to 1985. DHS informed this man that "[a]lthough you no longer belong to the Iranian National Resistance Movement, your actions in support of the organization constitute engaging in terrorism by providing material support of a terrorist organization." Most Iranians who lived through the early 1980's, and no doubt remember prior U.S. support for the Shah's regime, would be surprised to learn that the U.S. government now considers the printing and distribution of Iranian monarchist propaganda to be "terrorist activity." Most Americans would also be surprised to learn that the Department of Homeland Security considers the immigration law's definition of "terrorist activity" to extend to the publication of political materials without regard for their content.[62]

In denying permanent residence to a refugee from Ethiopia who had previously been granted asylum, DHS cited as "material support" to the Oromo Liberation Front (OLF) the applicant's statements that while still in Ethiopia he had circulated publications prepared by Oromos abroad. [63] One of the publications the applicant listed, *The Oromo Commentary*, is an academic journal, which publishes articles such as "Religion, the Slave Trade and the Creation of the Ethiopian Empire in the Nineteenth Century," and "Reasons for Choosing the Latin Script for Developing an Oromo Alphabet." Another, *The Kindling Point*, a series of pamphlets published by an Oromo exile living in the United States, consisted of personal reflections on Oromo national identity and the situation of the Oromo in Ethiopia. [64] (A representative essay in this series, for example, described how the author, an Oromo Christian, as a young man came to question and ultimately reject the traditional prohibition that prevented Christians in Ethiopia from eating meat slaughtered by Muslims, and vice versa.)[65]

In the case of applications for permanent residence and family reunification pending before DHS service centers—where DHS adjudicators considering those applications are rereading the applications for asylum or refugee status that DHS or the immigration court system had previously granted—DHS has at times treated any use of the word "support" to mean that the applicant provided "material support" to a group.

> Fatmushe, who is an ethnic Albanian woman from Kosovo, is 76 years old and was granted asylum years ago. In her application for asylum, after discussing her family's membership in and political activities in support of the Democratic League of Kosovo, she stated: "My family and I have supported also the Mother Teresa Humanitarian Association and the Kosova Liberation Army, KLA for our freedom and liberty after Feb. 98." In February 2008, DHS denied her application for permanent residence on the grounds that she had provided "material support" to the KLA and that the KLA was an undesignated "terrorist organization." The above statement quoted from her written application for asylum was the only evidence provided that she had "supported" the KLA. Fatmushe filed a motion to reopen with the Nebraska Service Center, together with an affidavit in which she made clear that her "support" for the KLA referred only to her political opinion—she did not give them

> money or anything else. While her case was reopened as nearly all of these denied adjustment cases were as a result of administrative advocacy, congressional pressure, and media attention later that spring, the arguments in her motion to reopen were ignored and her case was placed back on hold where it remains to this day.[66]

While Human Rights First is hopeful that DHS, when it finally readjudicates Fatmushe's case, will ultimately recognize that no bar applies, DHS has generally not been revisiting these adjustment cases until it implements waivers for the categories of cases into which DHS believes they fall. The result for people like Fatmushe is that their motions and explanations go unattended, unless they sue DHS in federal court to force adjudication of their cases, as an increasing number of increasingly frustrated applicants have been doing.

In another case involving an older woman whose application for asylum is still pending, however, the Department of Homeland Security has maintained that a "terrorism bar" applies, even though the facts in the record show only emotional support and family loyalty:

> Aashaa, a member of the Oromo ethnic group and a citizen of Ethiopia, is the mother of a large family whose husband was active in the political activities of the Oromo Liberation Front (OLF) during the period 1991-1992 when the OLF was part of the transitional government of Ethiopia. Shortly before the OLF withdrew from the government, Aashaa's husband was shot and killed by members of the ruling party. Aashaa herself is not and has never been a member of the OLF. Her late husband was, several of her brothers were or are still, and one of her children later joined the party, but Aashaa herself did not. Although she saw the OLF as representative of the aspirations of the Oromo people, her support for that cause was purely emotional. She never gave any tangible support to the OLF. Yet her application for asylum has been on hold for three years.

> In the period of political repression that followed Aashaa's husband's murder, one of her sons and a daughter disappeared. Aashaa later heard that her daughter had sought refuge with OLF soldiers in a remote area, from which she never returned, to Aashaa's lasting sorrow. Her son, then a child, went into hiding but was caught and jailed for months; Aashaa only learned this when the boy emerged from deten-

tion. When her son was later arrested again for political reasons, Aashaa visited him in jail and brought him food and drink since the jail did not provide this. On a later occasion when her son was again detained arbitrarily for his peaceful political activities, Aashaa provided money for a bribe to get her son released from jail. At one point, after her missing daughter had been gone for several years, men came to Aashaa and told her that her daughter needed money for transportation to come home. Desperate to see her daughter again, Aashaa gave them money and food. These men turned out to be Ethiopian government agents, who arrested her. This was one of several incidents of arrest, detention, and beating that Aashaa endured over the years. An easy target, left unprotected as she tried to bring up her younger children, Aashaa was made to suffer for the political activities of the rest of her family. Finally unable to bear this any longer, Aashaa fled to the United States. She was forced to leave behind her remaining children, several of whom are still of elementary or middle-school age. Aashaa says she has been missing her children for so long that she no longer feels "like a normal human being." She cannot hope for reunification with them until her application for asylum is approved. [67]

Although her family ties caused Aashaa to suffer repeated arrest and mistreatment at the hands of the Ethiopian government over a period of many years, they do not make her inadmissible to the United States. Aashaa herself never did anything to land in terrorism-bar limbo, other than marry, be widowed, have children, and try to keep her family alive and together under extremely difficult circumstances. Her application for asylum has been on hold for three years because she fed her son while he was in jail.

Redefining Medical Care As "Material Support"

"If the provision of medical care were to be considered 'material support' under the INA, the result would be that healthcare workers would be required to deny medical care to certain wounded persons. Under such a reading of the INA healthcare workers would be in the untenable position of deciding whether a life is worth saving, whether a person has committed a crime or terrorist act, and whether a group should be denied medical treatment—a form of political decision-making incompatible with medical ethics and international law."

Physicians for Human Rights (September 19, 2007)[68]

Doctors and other medical workers have also had their applications for refugee protection or permanent residence in the United States denied or placed on indefinite hold based on their own statements that they provided medical care to sick or wounded people who belonged to various non-state armed groups. Some of these medical workers—like Mariana, the Colombian nurse profiled earlier, and B.T., the Nepalese medic whose case is described below—were actually kidnapped by armed groups that forced them to treat their sick or wounded. Others treated these patients because they believed themselves to be obligated by principles of medical ethics to treat the sick and wounded without discrimination.[69] All of these applicants have seen their exercise of their professional duties redefined as "material support" to terrorism.

B.T. was initially granted asylum and withholding of removal by the immigration court in 2005, over DHS claims that his having been forced at gunpoint to provide emergency medical care to Maoist rebels who had kidnapped him, constituted "material support" to terrorism. The Board of Immigration Appeals upheld DHS's appeal in that respect. In an unpublished decision issued in September 2008, the BIA held that duress was legally irrelevant. The BIA held that B.T.'s additional argument, that medical care did not constitute "material support" and that to find otherwise would have serious implications for medical ethics and medical neutrality, was simply another form of a duress claim.[70] Although B.T. was found to be eligible for asylum but for the "material support" issue and thus eligible to be considered for a waiver of the bar by DHS, it took nearly four years after the immigration judge first granted him asylum for DHS to give him a waiver. (The dysfunctions of the process by which DHS considers waivers in removal cases are described in Part 6 of this report.)

While those, like B.T., who acted under threat of violence, will be considered for an exercise of DHS's waiver authority as people who acted under duress, DHS's waiver authority has offered no solution to those who did so voluntarily in accordance with their ethical obligations as medical workers.

The characterization of medical care as "material support" to terrorism is incompatible with core principles of medical ethics. It is also inconsistent with customary international law, which requires that those principles be respected in situations of armed conflict; that the sick and the wounded be treated humanely; and that healthcare workers not be penalized for performing medical duties consistent with medical ethics.[71] In keeping with these principles, the United States military instructs its personnel on their obligation to provide humane treatment and care to wounded and sick persons who fall into their hands, without regard to their political affiliation.[72] The Department of Defense in 2006 reaffirmed that these same principles apply to all detainees in the control of the Armed Forces, suspected terrorists included.[73]

The same logic that treats medical care to wounded combatants as "material support" also underlies attacks against healthcare workers that the U.S. government has rightly condemned when they take place in other countries. During the war in Kosovo, for example, Serbian forces killed, tortured, detained, and caused the disappearance of Kosovar Albanian physicians who treated members of the Kosovo Liberation Army. The U.S. State Department in its annual human rights report listed this as a violation of international law. The State Department had the same reaction when Russian forces opened fire on doctors and other medical workers at a hospital in Chechnya, and when Colombian paramilitaries declared doctors and hospitals suspected of treating guerrillas to be "military targets."[74]

Respect for the principle of medical neutrality is critical to allow parties to armed conflicts to fulfill their legal obligations toward the wounded and the sick, and to allow doctors and other medical workers to perform their medical duties without fear of attack. Failing to honor this principle sends a message that has dangerous implications for the safety of medical workers—including those working with U.S. forces—in war zones around the world, as well as for the health of the patients they seek to treat.

Your Mama's a Terrorist—Inadmissibility by Blood and Marriage

"You are the child of an inadmissible alien. For that reason, you are inadmissible . . ."

> Letters sent to numerous asylee and refugee children
> by the Department of Homeland Security
> (February/March 2008)

In one of its cruelest and most unnecessary strokes, the REAL ID Act made inadmissible—and thus barred from refugee protection as well as permanent residence—the spouses and children of people deemed to be inadmissible under any of the "terrorism"-related provisions of the immigration law based on activities that occurred within the past five years.[75] This provision is punishing the children, husbands, and wives of people many of whom are themselves only inadmissible based on questionable interpretations of the "terrorism bars." It has denied permanent residence, for example, to the minor daughter of a woman who suffered atrocious harm due to her peaceful political activities as a member of a group the Department of Homeland security considers to be a "Tier III terrorist organization:"

Hawa, a member of the Oromo ethnic group in Ethiopia, was granted asylum based on the persecution she suffered there due to her political activities as an active member of the Oromo Liberation Front (OLF). Hawa was a leader of the OLF women's group in the area where she lived; her activities as described in her asylum application consisted in discussing women's issues, recruiting new members, and fundraising. For these activities Hawa was arrested and imprisoned without charges. She was beaten, whipped with electrical cables, and stomped on until she signed a "confession." She was also raped at gunpoint by one of her interrogators. She believes it was as a result of this rape that she became infected with HIV, as her husband was HIV-negative. Hawa escaped to the United States with her youngest child; her husband and other children joined her here after she was granted asylum. She described all the facts above in her application for asylum, and her case was granted on that basis by an immigration judge after a full adversarial proceeding. The whole family then applied for permanent residence. In early 2008, all of their applications were denied. Hawa was denied based on the same activities as a member of the OLF that had led her to be granted asylum at a time when the provisions of law now invoked to deny her permanent residence were already on the books. Her daughter, a minor child, received a denial letter stating: "You are the child of an inadmissible alien. For that reason, you are inadmissible . . ."[76]

Hawa and her family are not isolated examples. In early 2008, a 14-year-old boy from Sudan received a letter from the Department of Homeland Security deeming him to be inadmissible on "terrorism" grounds and denying his application for permanent residence based on the fact that his mother was a member of the democratic opposition in Sudan.[77] Entire families of Sudanese asylees and refugees have likewise been denied permanent residence based on the democratic activism of a parent or spouse.[78]

A mother from Ethiopia was denied permanent residence together with her four children based on her political activism in the Ethiopian People's Revolutionary Party (EPRP), which she had joined in 1989.[79] In this case and in several others, DHS issued denials of permanent residence to asylees who were presently or formerly associated with the EPRP, denial letters that referred to acts of violence by the EPRP in the late 1970's and early 1980's, before many of these asylees had been associated with the group. A woman whose husband had joined the EPRP in 1998 was denied permanent residence on that basis.[80]

These cases were ultimately reopened by DHS following public concern and media attention, but remain on hold, and neither parents nor children have any way of knowing how long it will be before their requests for permanent residence are approved.

5. The Failure to Deal with the Crisis: The Waiver Morass

"The present interpretation of the material support bar has effectively altered U.S. policy so that refugees and asylum seekers who have suffered at the hands of terrorists and despotic regimes are no longer welcome to the U.S. as our friends."

Letter to President Bush from religious groups including the National Association of Evangelical Churches, the Southern Baptist Ethics and Religious Liberty Commission, the National Council of Churches of Christ, the Religious Action Center of Reform Judaism, the U.S. Conference of Catholic Bishops, and other groups (August 24, 2006) [81]

Concept and Statutory Background of the Waiver

When it last broadened the "terrorism"-related provisions of the immigration laws in 2005, as part of the REAL ID Act, Congress also gave the Secretaries of State and Homeland Security discretionary authority to decline to apply these provisions in particular cases or to particular Tier III "terrorist organizations." Under this statutory provision, codified at section 212(d)(3)(B) of the Immigration and Nationality Act (8 U.S.C. § 1182(d)(3)(B)), the Secretary of State exercises this authority over persons who are abroad, and the Secretary of Homeland Security over persons in the United States, both acting in consultation with the Attorney General.

This authority is commonly referred to as a "waiver" provision. From an immigration law perspective, this term is something of a misnomer. The 212(d)(3) "waiver" authority does not require that a person first be found to be subject to one of the "terrorism"-related bars before being granted a waiver of its application. The process that the relevant agencies have devised to grant waivers of the "terrorism bars" also does not include the features commonly associated with waivers of other inadmissibility grounds that are a standard feature of immigration practice, namely notice to the person affected that he or she has been found to be inadmissible, and a procedure to apply for a waiver. Despite these anomalies, this report uses the term "waiver" to refer to the discretionary

authority not to apply the "terrorism"-related inadmissibility grounds of the immigration law, because it has come into common use in public discussion in the years since its enactment.

The waiver authority enacted as part of the REAL ID Act replaced earlier discretionary authority that had been included in the USA PATRIOT Act and vested in the Attorney General. That earlier discretionary authority applied only to the "material support" bar, and had been codified as part of the immigration law's material support provisions. [82] As far as Human Rights First is aware, it was never used from the time of its enactment in 2001 until it was superseded in 2005 by the new REAL ID Act waiver authority, even as the backlog of cases on hold for "material support" reasons grew during those years.

Throughout 2005 and 2006, it became clear that the expansive application of the "terrorism bars" was threatening to shut down the U.S. refugee resettlement program and causing undeserved problems to increasing numbers of asylum seekers in the United States. By the summer of 2006, the Department of Homeland Security had placed on hold over 565 applications for asylum and about 700 applications for permanent residence filed by people already granted asylum or refugee status. [83] A diverse array of refugee advocacy organizations and religious and political groups expressed concern, as did members of Congress. The media reported on the issue and published editorials recommending action.

In response, the Departments of Justice and Homeland Security pointed to the REAL ID Act's waiver provisions as their preferred means of mitigating both the overbreadth of the immigration law's definitions of "terrorist activity" and "terrorist organization," and the effects of those agencies' own increasingly extreme interpretations of those and other "terrorism"-related provisions in the immigration context. Both agencies argued that this was what Congress had intended.[84] The fact that the statute made waivers discretionary and unreviewable was a major factor in the executive agencies' preference for this approach.[85]

Failure of Implementation

The Glacial Pace of Waiver Announcements and the Failure to Implement a Process to Grant Waivers in Removal Proceedings

"[D]enying refugees admission to the United States because they were physically forced against their will to assist a terrorist organization, or because they provided inconsequential support to organizations which oppose particularly oppressive regimes, is not only undermining the leadership of the United States in the field of human rights, it is endangering the lives of innocent refugees who have fled terror or repression."

U.S. Commission on International Religious Freedom (May 1, 2006)[86]

Unfortunately, inter-agency attempts to implement the discretionary waiver authority quickly made clear why a process that requires consultation among three Cabinet-level officials is not a realistic method of conducting refugee status determinations and other routine immigration adjudications.

Hesitant to delegate their statutory authority to waive application of the "terrorism bars" to the adjudicators actually deciding asylum and refugee cases, the Secretary of State

and the DHS Secretary began to implement this broad statutory authority in a very limited, piecemeal fashion, through periodic announcements allowing adjudicators to exercise that authority with respect to the particular categories of cases covered by these Secretarial announcements. These announcements proceeded extremely slowly.

It took nearly a year of meetings and inter-agency discussions from the time the REAL ID Act's waiver provision was enacted in 2005 before the Secretary of State was able to issue the first of these waiver announcements. That May 2006 waiver announcement was issued to allow the resettlement of one large group of Burmese refugees from the Karen ethnic group who were then living in one particular refugee camp in Thailand and had provided support to the Karen National Union, a political movement of Burma's Karen ethnic minority whose army engaged in combat against Burmese military forces. That first waiver announcement was extended in August 2006 to cover Karen refugees in other locations in Thailand. These waivers for refugees overseas—much needed and welcome though they were to the Karen refugees affected—had no effect on similarly-situated refugees seeking asylum from within the United States. It was not until January 2007 that the Secretary of Homeland Security issued an announcement allowing Karen refugees seeking asylum in the United States who had given to the Karen National Union to benefit from the same exemption granted months earlier to their compatriots in Thailand who had done exactly the same thing.[87]

Waiver announcements by the Secretary of State followed in January 2007 for refugees overseas who had given to a series of other groups whose new categorization as "terrorist organizations" had attracted the notice of policy-makers and the media, both because this categorization was blocking the resettlement of populations of refugees who had been slated for imminent resettlement to the United States, and because these newly defined "terrorist organizations" were groups that were seen as friendly to (or had actually been allied with) the United States.[88] The new announcements covered several other Burmese groups that fought the military junta in that country (the Karenni National Progressive Party, the Kayan New Land Party, the Chin National Front, the Chin National

League for Democracy, the Arakan Liberation Party), the Mustangs (a reference to a Tibetan group that had fought the Chinese takeover of Tibet), and the Alzados (short for *Alzados en armas*, this term refers to Cubans who had rebelled against the Castro regime in the 1960's, some of whose supporters now found themselves blocked from expected resettlement in the United States).[89]

The announcements of waivers of the "material support" bar for contributors to these groups overseas were followed by parallel announcements by the Secretary of Homeland Security. The practical impact on asylum seekers in the United States, however, was limited by two factors. First, relatively few asylum seekers in the United States had been associated with these particular groups. Although Burmese ethnic minorities made up a significant proportion of the overseas refugee caseload that the U.S. had committed itself to resettling out of Thailand and Malaysia before the "terrorism bars" emerged as a problem, there were not that many members of these populations applying for asylum from within the United States. The population of refugees seeking asylum in the U.S. is more diverse than the overseas refugee resettlement caseload, and includes different groups of refugees. Most of the asylum cases that were on hold with the Asylum Office, or running into difficulties before the immigration courts and the Board of Immigration Appeals due to the "terrorism bars," were cases that involved duress at the hands of armed groups (many of them Tier I or Tier II groups) or voluntary association with a much broader range of groups now considered to fall into the Tier III definition.

Second, a significant proportion of the Burmese asylum seekers in the United States who *were* covered by the substantive scope of these waiver announcements were unable to benefit from a waiver because their cases were pending before the immigration courts, the Board of Immigration Appeals, or the federal courts, rather than before the Asylum Office. And the Departments of Homeland Security and Justice had not yet implemented any procedure to allow cases in removal proceedings to be considered for a waiver of the "material support" bar. One Burmese Chin applicant, for example, was detained for months, even after DHS's implementation of a waiver of the material support bar

for voluntary contributions to the Chin National Front, because there was no process in place to allow him to be granted such a waiver in removal proceedings.[90]

In addition to these gaps in implementation of the statutory waiver authority that existed at that time, the statute itself did not give the Secretaries of State and Homeland Security the authority to grant waivers to certain categories of people. Anyone who had actually taken part in "terrorist activity" himself—which, in practice, meant anyone who had actually fought with a non-state armed group, including groups that had fought with U.S. forces during the war in Vietnam—was not eligible for a waiver even under the statute as it had been enacted in 2005.

Statutory Expansion of Waiver Authority

"We cannot under current legislative authority exempt from the application of the bar aliens who were actual combatants under arms, and this accounts for our failure to provide relief to many of the Hmong and Montagnards who fought beside our troops in Vietnam, as well as to some of the child soldiers who are the subject of your earlier hearing. . . The administration sent forward a legislative proposal to fix this gap. . . With respect to how to speed up the process and hold our feet to the fire, well, this hearing certainly helps."

Paul Rosenzweig, Deputy Assistant Secretary for Policy, DHS, September 19, 2007[91]

"[W]hat we want to make sure is that when lives are at risk, we go full speed forward and we do not use the idea of doing what is safe when we can do what is right. . . We are going to work, Senator Durbin and I have committed to work to get the legislative changes that you need. But I think we need to hear from you a commitment that this is a priority, we are going to do it, because every life that is hanging out there that we do not make a positive impact on is a life that is going to be lost or wasted."

Sen. Tom Coburn, September 19, 2007[92]

The Bush Administration asked Congress to fill the gaps in the existing statutory waiver authority, assuring lawmakers that an expansion of its discretionary authority would allow resolution of the full range of asylum and refugee cases that were the focus of public concern. With bipartisan support, Congress responded to the Bush Administration's call for expanded waiver authority and in December 2007 amended the Secretaries' waiver authority so that it could now cover all of the immigration law's "terrorism"-related bars, with the exception of voluntary association with or support to groups listed or designated by the State Department as terrorist organizations (Tier I or Tier II groups).[93]

Through the same legislation, Congress provided that 10 named groups that had been deemed to be "Tier III" terrorist organizations under the immigration law should no longer be considered such based on anything they had done prior to the passage of that amending legislation. The 10 groups in question were groups that had arisen primarily in the context of overseas refugee resettlement, and whose characterization as "terrorist organizations" many in Congress had found particularly disturbing. Six were Burmese groups (the Karen National Union/Karen Liberation Army, the Chin National Front/Chin National Army, the Chin National League for Democracy, the Kayan New Land Party, the Arakan Liberation Party, and the Karenni National Progressive Party). The others were the Mustangs from Tibet, the Alzados in Cuba, and "appropriate groups affiliated with the Hmong and the Montagnards." All of these groups had already been the object of material support waiver announcements by the Secretaries of State and Homeland Security.

Renewed Failure of Implementation: Unexpected Denial of Permanent Residence to Hundreds of Refugees

"For three years I had not smoked, and now I'm smoking."

> Iraqi refugee, describing psychological impact of being denied permanent residence based on his past affiliation with an armed group opposed to the Saddam Hussein regime

When Congress expanded DHS's waiver authority at the end of 2007, refugees and their advocates hoped that the situation would improve. Instead, in January 2008, DHS suddenly began to deny hundreds of refugees' applications for permanent residence and family reunification, applications that the agency had previously placed on hold based on the "terrorism"-related provisions of the immigration law. All of these applications had been filed by people who had already been granted asylum or refugee status. Some of them had been pending for years; others had been filed more recently. Virtually all were eligible to be considered for waivers under DHS's expanded statutory waiver authority; most could also have been issued waivers under the previous version of the statute.

However, then-DHS Secretary Michael Chertoff had not yet taken steps to implement that statutory waiver authority. In the absence of any clear indication as to when such implementation might happen, U.S. Citizenship & Immigration Services suddenly began to deny cases that were eligible for waivers under the statute but were not covered by any of the exemption announcements made up to that point. These denials, over 600 of which were sent out between January and March 2008, sowed panic in refugee households and communities across the country.

"They say I am a terrorist! They are trying to deport me!"

> Identical exclamation of multiple refugees and asylees, summarizing letters they had just received from DHS denying them permanent residence, February 2008

The denial letters were the first indication most of these applicants received that DHS believed that there was a "terrorism"-related problem with their cases. The shock and confusion they created were magnified by several factors. First, the letters were incomprehensible. Or rather, the essential message their recipients grasped was clear enough—the U.S. government considered them to be terrorists. But the factual basis for this determination was often incoherently presented, the actual practical implications for the recipients were nowhere explained, there was no reference to the statutory availability of a waiver under section 212(d)(3) of the Immigration & Nationality Act, and there was no explanation of what applicants who believed the denials were wrong could do about it. (A redacted example of one of these denial letters is reproduced at Appendix C.) Second, DHS was denying these applicants permanent residence based on the same information they had themselves provided in their applications for asylum and refugee status, which had already been approved years ago.

These asylees and refugees fell into two categories: Those who had been granted refugee protection (in the form of asylum or refugee resettlement) before the enactment of the statutory provisions that were now being invoked to deny them permanent residence, and those who had been granted refugee protection under a version of the statute that was the same in all relevant respects to the one currently in force. An Eritrean man who had fought for his country's independence before becoming a critic of its new government fell into the first of these two groups:

> Berhane joined the Eritrean People's Liberation Front (EPLF) and fought in the EPLF's war for independence from Ethiopia for several years in the 1970's, until he was severely wounded in battle. Eritrea became independent in 1993, and the political successor to the EPLF became the ruling party, which continues to rule Eritrea to this day. After independence, Berhane was targeted for persecution by the Eritrean government for his peaceful political activities and connections to other political dissidents who were concerned at their government's increasingly authoritarian tendencies. Berhane fled Eritrea after being tipped off that he was about to be arrested as a dissident. He applied for asylum in the United States in 2002 and was granted. In 2008, he received a letter denying him permanent residence on the grounds that having fought for Eritrean independence in the 1970's constituted having "engaged in terrorist activity" under a U.S. statute enacted in 1990. That "terrorist activity" definition had already been in force for a dozen years when Berhane had been granted asylum after disclosing these same facts.[94]

Other applicants who fought decades ago for the independence of countries now long established and internationally recognized also saw their applications for permanent residence denied under the same statute that had previously granted them asylum.

Sachin Karmakar, a longstanding advocate for the rights of religious minorities in Bangladesh, was granted asylum in the United States on political and religious grounds. He subsequently applied for permanent residence. In early 2008, DHS informed him that it intended to deny his application based on the fact that in 1971, as a young student, he had fought in his country's battle for independence from Pakistan. The Bangladeshi nationalist movement was subject to bloody but ultimately unsuccessful repression by the Pakistani Army; hundreds of thousands of Bangladeshis are estimated to have been killed, including a large number of civilians. Members of the country's Hindu minority were particular targets; Mr. Karmakar's father, who was Hindu, was one of those killed. Pakistani forces surrendered less than nine months later. Bangladesh has, obviously, been a recognized nation since that time. In the words of the U.S. Department of State, "U.S.-Bangladesh friendship and support developed quickly following Bangladesh's independence from Pakistan in 1971. U.S-Bangladesh relations are excellent."[95]

Adding to the general sense of arbitrariness, nearly all of the asylees and refugees who received these denials knew other people similarly situated—friends, relatives, compatriots in their communities—who had previously been granted asylum or refugee status and/or permanent residence (and in some cases later U.S. citizenship) without problems after declaring the same kinds of activities and associations. In some cases, within the same family, some were denied, while others, whose applications had been processed slightly earlier, were granted, without there having been any intervening change in law. The same is true of asylum applicants whose requests for protection are being derailed by the "terrorism bars."

A recent news article described the case of Tsegu Bahta, an Eritrean national who had fought for Eritrean independence from Ethiopia. He had gone on to serve as a high official of the new Eritrean government and to work for reform, only to come under increasing suspicion from the Eritrean authorities. He fled to the United States, where he had ties, and applied for asylum, only to find that his past work with the Eritrean People's Liberation Front now defined him as a "terrorist" according to the Department of Homeland Security. This man's uncle, meanwhile, had likewise joined the struggle for Eritrean independence, had chaired the new nation's Constitutional Commission, and also later became a vocal critic of the Eritrean government. The uncle is a U.S. citizen and a professor of law at the University of North Carolina at Chapel Hill.[96]

DHS, in the face of inquiries from congressional committees, initially showed little interest in reversing these decisions, although it did agree to place a moratorium on issuing further denials to allow DHS to review the process. The agency reversed course after the *Washington Post* published an article (on its front page and on Easter Sunday, 2008), describing how DHS had denied permanent residence to Saman Kareem Ahmad, an Iraqi interpreter for the U.S. Marine Corps—who at the time he received this denial was working as an instructor for the Marines at Quantico—based on the fact that he had formerly received "military-type training" from an Iraqi Kurdish group which had fought alongside U.S. forces to overthrow the government of Saddam Hussein.[97]

DHS then agreed to reopen the cases previously denied, and did reopen virtually all of them, with the exception of a few cases found to be ineligible for permanent residence on unrelated grounds. Since that time DHS has been processing those that became eligible for waiver consideration pursuant to announcements made by the Secretary of Homeland Security in late 2008: people deemed to have provided "material support" under duress to listed or designated (Tier I/II) groups, and people who had fought (or had certain other types of associations with) one of the 10 groups removed from the Tier III definition by the congressional action at the end of 2007. But the rest of the applications for permanent residence or family reunification filed by refugees and asylees that had been denied in early 2008, or were still on hold at that time, remain on hold to this day. And the number of these stalled applications continues to grow, as waiver implementation has failed to keep pace with the expanding application of the "terrorism bars" themselves. Most of these applicants, who currently number over 7,000, are people who had had voluntary connections to groups or armed struggles that are now believed to fall within the immigration law's sweeping "Tier III" definition.[98]

"They say I am a terrorist—but they don't want to deport me?"

> Asylee from Afghanistan, identifying a paradox central to the "terrorism-bars" debate

One of the many ironies of the expanding terrorism-bar morass is that the overwhelming majority of those affected by this crisis are people whom no one—not even the Department of Homeland Security—actually considers to pose a threat to the security of the United States. Even as it was sending out letters denying permanent residence to asylees and refugees early last year, DHS was indicating in no uncertain terms to refugee advocates and congressional staffers that it had no plans to touch those refugees' underlying refugee or asylum status simply because it believed them to be subject to a "terrorism"-related ground of inadmissibility under present law. Indeed, in order to keep a person's case on "hold" based on the immigration law's "terrorism bars," DHS must believe that the person does *not* pose a danger to the United States—this is a requirement of the agency's "hold" policy. The person must also be eligible for the benefit he is applying for and not be subject to any other bars.[99]

Back in Alice in Wonderland: A Tale of Two Iraqis

The one person to be extracted from "voluntary Tier III" limbo in 2008-2009 was Saman Kareem Ahmad, the Iraqi former interpreter, now language and culture instructor, for the U.S. Marine Corps, who was granted an individual waiver of inadmissibility promptly after he was profiled on the front page of the *Washington Post* in late March 2008. Right around the same time as Saman Kareem, another Iraqi Kurd who had worked as an interpreter for U.S. forces received a nearly identical denial of his application for permanent residence.

> A member of Iraq's Kurdish ethnic minority, Talal worked for the Kurdish Democratic Party (KDP) before 2005. He later worked as a linguist and translator for U.S. armed forces. He received extensive support and commendation from the U.S. officers he worked with for performing the "highest quality" of linguistic support despite the "obvious risk to life and limb" and a "substantial amount of personal sacrifice and risk exposure."

According to his superiors, he "served tirelessly alongside U.S. soldiers and civilians and his allegiance, sincerity and ethics are beyond reproach." Like many interpreters and other Iraqis who worked with U.S. forces, Talal's life was threatened in Iraq, and he sought protection in the United States. He was granted asylum by an Immigration Judge after full disclosure of his past association with the KDP. He then went on to apply for permanent residence. In early 2008, his application for permanent residence was denied on the grounds that because he was "involved with the Kurdish Democratic Party (KDP) and worked for the KDP voluntarily, prior to January 30, 2005, when the KDP became part of the Kurdistan National Government," he had committed "acts of material support to the KDP," a group which "meets the current definition of an undesignated terrorist organization." The denial letter explained that "KDP rebels conducted full-scale armed attacks and helped to incite rebellions against [Saddam] Hussein's regime, most notably during the Iran-Iraq war, Operation Desert Storm, and Operation Iraqi Freedom." DHS reopened Talal's case along with nearly all the over 600 cases it had denied around the same time, but unlike Saman Kareem's, Talal's case has remained on hold since that time.

At a Congressional hearing shortly after the media coverage of Saman Kareem's case, DHS Secretary Chertoff told Senator Leahy, "With respect to Mr. Ahmad, the translator, I waived the objection to his getting a green card yesterday, so we're out of Alice in Wonderland."[100] Secretary Chertoff's comment, unfortunately, masked the continuing reality that the only applicant to have emerged from Wonderland was Saman Kareem Ahmad—every other person in his situation, no matter how similarly situated, was still stuck in the land of the March Hare.

The reason Saman Kareem was able to be named and photographed in a media account of his situation was that his entire family had been killed by Saddam Hussein's gas attacks on the Kurds at Halabja in the 1980's. As of the publication of this report, however, Talal cannot let his name appear in print because he fears for the lives of relatives who are still in Iraq.

Although the memoranda and worksheets DHS issued to its staff on implementing its waiver authority make reference to the possibility of granting individual waivers, those same documents contemplate that any such individual waivers would need to be granted by the Secretary of Homeland Security him- or herself. In practice, the DHS Secretary has not exercised that option. While Saman Kareem's situation was resolved, Talal was left to wait for another year and a half for a broader DHS waiver announcement for persons associated with the KDP.[101]

6. The Crisis Continues

"The law needs reform, and not just to make more groups eligible for waivers."

Editorial, "Punishing Refugees Twice," *New York Times*, September 23, 2006

Four and a half years after the passage of the REAL ID Act, and eight years after the enactment of the USA PATRIOT Act, legitimate refugees who pose no threat to the United States continue to suffer from the impact of overly broad definitions in the immigration laws that were intended to protect the United States against terrorism. Despite four years of bipartisan congressional concern and the change in Administration, there also has not yet been any discernible change in federal agencies' interpretation of the immigration law's "terrorism"-related provisions.

Nearly two years ago Congress attempted to address the impact of these provisions through piecemeal statutory changes, responding to the immigration agencies' request for broader authority to grant unreviewable discretionary "waivers." But that waiver authority—originally described as a tool for flexibility—has instead proved to be an instrument of paralysis. Where waiver authority has been implemented, U.S. Citizenship & Immigration Services is now adjudicating cases eligible for waivers that have already been imple-mented, although the process remains duplicative and is not transparent. But with the exception of group-specific waivers for three Iraqi groups, there have been no announcements of further waivers since the end of 2008. And the waivers for these three Iraqi groups, finally announced in late October 2009, had been under consideration by DHS, the Depart-ment of Justice, and the Department of State since early 2008. Meanwhile, a total of over 7,500 cases pending with the Department of Homeland Security were on indefinite hold as of September 2009 based on actual or perceived issues relating to the immigration law's "terrorism"-related provi-sions. The number of applications for permanent residence and family reunification filed by asylees and refugees (all

previously granted protection) newly placed on hold by DHS increased by 1,423 between March and September of 2009.

Asylum seekers who are in immigration court proceedings, who may face actual deportation to countries where they fear persecution and thus have an urgent claim to the U.S. government's attention under the Refugee Convention and Protocol, continue to face the greatest obstacles in being considered for discretionary waivers. As detailed below, the process to consider waivers in immigration court cases, finally announced in October 2008, is cumbersome, ineffective, and plagued by delay. In addition, that process only applies to refugees who were subject to duress or were involved with the limited number of "Tier III" groups whose members and associates have benefited from group-specific waivers. Those applicants eligible under the statute for waivers that have not yet been announced are left out of this process altogether, as DHS Immigration & Customs Enforcement continues to move their cases forward down the road to deportation.

Still Expanding the Law's Overbreadth: Administrative Interpretation of the "Terrorism Bars"

Nine months into the Obama Administration, immigration adjudicators at the Department of Homeland Security and the Department of Justice, and lawyers representing the Department of Homeland Security before the immigration courts and the Board of Immigration Appeals, are continuing to apply the problematic legal interpretations of the immigra-tion law's "terrorism" bars that were adopted by those departments over the past eight years. As described in greater detail in Part 2 of this report, these legal positions include:

■ Retroactive application of the USA PATRIOT Act's definition of an "undesignated" or "Tier III" organization to groups that no longer exist or that have given up violence;

■ Treating victims of armed groups as supporters of the groups that extorted goods or services from them under threat of violence;

■ Applying the "terrorism bars" to the acts of children in the same way as to adults, thereby barring a number of former child soldiers and child captives of armed groups;

■ Treating minimal contributions as "material support;"

■ Interpreting "material support" to cover virtually anything, including speech and other pure political activity, that a person did in connection with his or her membership in a group the Department of Homeland Security deems to be a "terrorist organization;"

■ Treating medical care as "material support."

Several of the most extreme examples of unduly expansive interpretation of the "terrorism bars" described earlier in this report were litigated (or are still being litigated) by DHS Immigration & Customs Enforcement in 2009.

> Louis, the Burundian asylum applicant profiled in Part 4 of this report, first learned in late 2008 that the Department of Homeland Security was deeming the robbery of his lunch and $4 by armed rebels to constitute "material support" to those same rebels. But the Department of Homeland Security proceeded to maintain that same position on appeal to the Board of Immigration Appeals in 2009, and on that basis refused to release Louis from the jails where he remained for a total of over 20 months, until the Board of Immigration Appeals overruled the Department of Homeland Security's legal position and granted his appeal in June 2009. Because this decision was unpublished, it is not binding on the Department of Homeland Security, which continues to treat minimal contributions as "material support."

Similarly, in a case described in further detail below, ICE continues to argue that an asylum applicant provided "material support" to a terrorist organization because armed members of the group abducted him and stood him in the middle of a road for hours, probably in the hope that he would serve as a human decoy to draw enemy fire. This case is still pending and the asylum applicant, who has been detained for over a year, remains in an immigration jail at the time of this writing.

Many other applications have remained on hold with U.S. Citizenship & Immigration Services based on the extreme interpretations of the immigration law's "terrorism"-related provisions discussed in detail in Part 4 of this report. These include several applications for asylum or permanent residence by doctors and other medical workers who provided medical care in accordance with their ethical obligations to wounded combatants and others whose activities brought them within the scope of the immigration law's "terrorism"-related provisions. Also still on hold are numerous cases involving minimal contributions that continue to be construed as "material support," cases where political activity and speech continues to be characterized as a ground of "terrorism"-related inadmissibility, as well as several cases where the "terrorism bars" continue to be applied to the actions of children.[102]

Still Waiting for Waivers of an Unworkable Legal Definition: The Continuing "Tier III" Problem

The government's highly centralized, controlled, and restrictive process for waiver implementation has proved to be no match for the entirely decentralized, uncontrolled, and expansive process by which government sub-agencies have been deeming groups to be "Tier III terrorist organizations," and deciding that individual asylum seekers and refugees are subject to "terrorism"-related bars. Implementing authority to grant waivers of the immigration law's "terrorism"-related provisions requires negotiations among the Departments of Homeland Security, State, and Justice, with the additional involvement of the National Security Council, and discussions among those agencies (and their various component agencies and offices) continue to consume time and resources out of all proportion to the practical results achieved—whether in providing relief to individual refugees or in advancing legitimate security objectives.

DHS's sudden issuance of denial letters to over 600 people with pending applications for permanent residence and family reunification in early 2008 (discussed in Part 5 of this report) first made clear just how far the immigration law's "terrorism"-related provisions were reaching, affecting applicants whom no one had previously classified in that way, and reaching back in time to groups that were now mainly of historical interest. For the rest of 2008, the Bush Administration proposed, and then failed to implement, a group-based approach to consider granting waivers to these people. Specifically, the Bush Administration's plan was to conduct an inter-agency review of each "Tier III terrorist organization" in order to determine whether to allow waivers for those affiliated with it. This was the same model that had been followed with a limited number of Burmese and other groups in 2006-2007.

But as detailed in Part 4 above, the number of groups that individual immigration adjudicators were deeming to be Tier III organizations was overwhelmingly large and constantly expanding. (Examples of groups found to fall into this category are listed in Part 3 above.)

The other difficulty with a scheme to "de-list" groups as Tier III organizations is that the Tier III definition does not require that groups be listed in the first place, and in fact discourages any such process. Tier I and Tier II organizations, the groups that are listed or designated as terrorist organizations and whose names appear on the State Department's website, are publicly declared to be Tier I or Tier II terrorist organizations as of the date that designation is made. The State Department notes that this public declaration, the notice it provides, and the stigmatizing and deterrent force it produces, is part of the point of defining a group as a terrorist organization.[103] Anyone who lends significant aid to such a group after its designation is liable for material support to a Tier I or Tier II organization under the immigration laws, and, in the case of a Tier I group, under the criminal laws as well. The public listing of the group provides notice of this fact, and

serves to discourage individuals from assisting the group in the future.

In the case of a Tier III group, however, the question under the statute is not only whether or not the group engages in violence, but whether the group was engaged in violence *at the time the applicant was associated with it.* This statutory definition poses major and unnecessary challenges for immigration adjudicators. The fact that the Tier III definition covers groups whose use of armed force has been quite minor and of no national-security significance to the U.S. government is part of what makes this difficult: the less significant a group's involvement in violent activity, the less documentation it generates. The decision by the Departments of State and Homeland Security to apply the Tier III definition backwards in time to groups that are no longer involved in violence only complicates both agencies' task in deciding immigration cases. Many of the decisions and filings Human Rights First has seen—from the DHS service centers that process applications for permanent residence and family reunification, and also from attorneys with DHS Immigration & Customs Enforcement (ICE) who represent DHS in immigration court—make vague and sometimes inaccurate reference to internet sources whose reliability and specificity varies widely. (Human Rights First has seen a number of DHS decisions and immigration court filings, for example, where the websites of groups that DHS considers to be "Tier III terrorist organizations" were cited as sources for the violent activities of *other* groups that DHS alleged fell under the "Tier III" definition.)

In practice, some DHS adjudicators appear to be solving this problem by ignoring chronology altogether, and relying on general statements about a group's activities whose sources are often unclear and that make no mention of relevant time periods. A young survivor of torture from Mauritania, for instance, whose application for permanent residence has been on hold for over five years now, recently learned that DHS considered him to have provided "material support" to a "Tier III terrorist organization" because of his limited and peaceful political involvement in the late 1990's with a group that had used armed force in the 1980's and early 1990's.

When Mohamed was 12 years old, all the members of his immediate family were expelled from their native Mauritania to Senegal. These expulsions were part of a campaign by the ruling military regime against Mauritania's black African ethnic groups, to which Mohamed's family belonged. Mohamed escaped expulsion because he was at the home of a relative when the police took his family away. Mohamed remained in Mauritania where he was cared for by relatives, with little news of his parents and siblings who were in a refugee camp in Senegal. As a young man, Mohamed became involved in FLAM (*Forces de Libération Africaines de Mauritanie*), through a friend of his who was an active member. Established in the early 1980's and swiftly outlawed in Mauritania, FLAM is an Afro-Mauritanian liberation movement that since the mid-1980's has operated mainly in exile. FLAM members had carried out a series of armed attacks inside Mauritania in 1986, causing little damage and no loss of life, but resulting in massive repression against anyone suspected of association with the group.[104] FLAM was also involved in armed cross-border attacks following the mass expulsions of black Mauritanians in 1989-90. All the sources Human Rights First has consulted, however, indicate that these attacks had ended by 1992.[105] Mohamed first became associated with FLAM in 1996. Mohamed was never actually a FLAM member, because his uncle impressed on him that this would be too dangerous for him and for the rest of their family. His activities in support of the group consisted in posting flyers at night that called on African Mauritanians to fight racial and ethnic discrimination, and in making minimal monetary contributions to FLAM. Mohamed was arrested, arbitrarily detained, and severely beaten on several occasions by Mauritanian security forces who believed that he was actually a member of FLAM. They interrogated him about his connections to group and about trips he had made to visit his family in exile in Senegal. Following his last detention, during which he was tortured, Mohamed fled to the United States. He was granted asylum in 2002.

In early 2004, Mohamed applied for permanent residence. Five years later, after Mohamed filed a petition in federal district court for a decision on his long-pending application, the Department of Homeland Security informed Mohamed for the first time that his case was on hold because it considered FLAM to be a "Tier III" terrorist organization, and considered Mohamed to have provided "material support" to FLAM.[106]

The statute is clear that the fact that a group is engaged in the use of armed force today does not make a person who gave to the group four years ago liable for material support if the group was non-violent at the time the person gave to it. Nor is a person liable under the statute for support provided to a group that was engaged in violent activities four years earlier but was not doing so at the time the support was provided. All of the agencies involved—the Department of Homeland Security, the Department of Justice, and the State Department—agree on this as a matter of legal interpretation, despite the chronological sloppiness that occurs in actual decision-making.[107] This makes it very difficult, and not very useful, to construct a "list" of Tier III organizations, and makes "de-listing" an unworkable approach to waiver implementation.

In fact, even Congress's attempts to force adjudication in favor of particular groups by enacting specific legislation on their behalf have failed fully to achieve that limited goal. Two years after Congress explicitly removed 10 groups from the "Tier III" definition in 2007, a number of applications for permanent residence or family reunification filed by refugees and asylees who had some association with the 10 named groups that Congress explicitly removed from the "Tier III" definition in 2007 remain on hold. A victim of severe religious and political persecution in Tibet, for example, has been unable to reunite with his wife and children:

> Dorjee's father and uncle fought with the Chushi Gangdruk, an organization of Tibetan guerrilla fighters who resisted the Chinese takeover of Tibet in the 1950's and 1960's. During that period, the Chushi Gangdruk received training and material support from the Central Intelligence Agency (CIA), and established a base in the Mustang region of neighboring Nepal. Dorjee's uncle was killed. His father was captured and spent the rest of his life in a Chinese labor camp. Dorjee, who was a child at the time of these events, never fought with the Chushi Gangdruk, which disarmed when Dorjee was a teenager. Dorjee himself was involved only in peaceful political and religious opposition to Chinese rule. For taking part in non-violent political demonstrations, Dorjee was arrested and tortured in the late 1980's-early 1990's. He continued with his activities after his release, distributing audio cassettes of songs in support of religious freedom. He fled the People's Republic of China after learning that the government was looking for him to arrest him again. He was granted asylum in the United States in 2006.

In 2007, Dorjee filed petitions to be reunited with his wife and children. In 2008, he filed an application for permanent residence. In 2007, Congress enacted legislation specifically stating that "the Mustangs" (i.e. the Tibetan guerrillas formerly based in the Nepalese Mustang region) should not be considered to be a "terrorist organization." The Chushi Gangdruk is what the Tibetan Mustang guerrillas called *themselves* in the days when they were guerrillas. The group long ago evolved into a non-violent social and cultural organization that supports the preservation of Tibetan culture and also maintains a retirement home in India for a number of very elderly survivors of the original Chushi Gangdruk and their families. In 2009, Dorjee was informed that his applications were on hold based on the immigration law's "terrorism"-related provisions. After his lawyer wrote to DHS Headquarters about the case, Dorjee's application for permanent residence was approved. But his petitions for his wife and children are still pending.[108]

An asylee from Laos has had the same experience, along with his wife and child, again despite the passage of legislation intended for their benefit:

> A member of the Hmong ethnic minority in Laos, Pao was part of the "secret army" recruited and trained by the Central Intelligence Agency (CIA) to fight on the U.S. side during the Vietnam War. When the U.S. withdrew in 1975, the Hmong became targets of persecution. Thousands fled as refugees to Thailand. In the late 1990's, the refugee camps where the Hmong refugees were living in Thailand were closed. Fearing persecution if they were forced to return to Laos, thousands were ultimately resettled in the United States as refugees, including Pao and his wife and child, who were brought to the United States in 2005. The family applied for permanent residence in 2008—after the passage of the law by which Congress specifically provided that "appropriate groups affiliated with the Hmong" should not be considered to be "a terrorist organization." Seven months after the passage of this legislation, the Department of Homeland Security issued a memorandum on its implementation that noted that "appropriate groups affiliated with the Hmong" would be understood to mean "ethnic Hmong individuals or groups" (provided there was no reason to believe that they had targeted non-combatants).[109] Yet nearly two years after the passage of legislation specifically intended to stop Hmong refugees like him from being characterized as "terrorists" under the immigration laws, Pao's application for permanent residence remains on hold, as do those of his wife and child.

By the beginning of 2009, it had become clear that proposals for a group-by-group approach to waivers for voluntary association with groups deemed to be Tier III organizations were not moving forward. Ten months later, the relevant agencies are still reviewing alternative approaches. In addition, implementation of waiver authority for other, smaller categories of cases was sidelined for much of 2009 pending resolution of the numerically larger "voluntary Tier III" category. For applicants in any of these categories, there has been hardly any progress in the past 19 months.

More Bumps in the Road: Notices of Intent to Terminate Asylum Status

In the summer of 2009 U.S. Citizenship & Immigration Services sent a small number of asylees notice that it intended to terminate their asylum status based on possible "terrorism"-bar concerns. USCIS scheduled these asylees for interviews on the possible revocation of their status. All were people whose requests for family reunification and/or permanent residence were on hold with USCIS, although most of the asylees in question did not know this at the time. The issuance of these asylum termination notices was particularly surprising since DHS officials had previously advised that the agency was *not* planning to revoke the asylum or refugee status of persons simply because their applications for family reunification or for permanent residence were flagged as subject to a possible "terrorism"-related bar.

When these concerns were raised with U.S. Citizenship & Immigration Services, the agency readily admitted that these "Notices of Intent to Terminate" had been a mistake, issued as a result of an internal miscommunication. USCIS stated that most of these asylees should expect that their asylum status would not be terminated—but that their applications for permanent residence or their petitions for their family would probably remain on hold. The Asylum Office indicated that it was sending most of the affected asylees notice that the agency would not be proceeding with the interviews that had previously been scheduled.[110] One asylee who had sought assistance from Human Rights First after receiving a

"Notice of Intent to Terminate" did then receive a letter from the Asylum Office, but this letter indicated that his scheduled interview was being cancelled "due to administrative problems" and would be rescheduled. The letter provided no explanation or background regarding the original decision to issue termination notices or the current decision to call them off. The letter was also inaccurate, in that the Asylum Office has stated that it does not plan to proceed with termination interviews in these cases unless it believes that asylum actually should be terminated based on the particular facts of the individual case. By the time that clarification was made, several of the affected asylees had already gone through "termination" interviews with the Asylum Office.

While this episode appears to have been a passing scare for most people as far as actual termination of asylum is concerned, the larger question is why these applicants' family petitions and permanent residence applications should have been placed on hold in the first place. In the cases Human Rights First has seen where asylees have received notices of intent to terminate their asylum status, asylum was granted within the past two years. At that time, DHS's understanding of the law had already reached its current interpretative expanse, and the law has not changed since. Nor did the applicants in question possess any characteristics that would seem likely to prompt particular adverse scrutiny.

Several, for example, are or were members of the Movement for Democratic Change (MDC) in Zimbabwe, a peaceful democratic opposition party in a country where the United States (among a great number of other countries) has repeatedly expressed encouragement for democratic reform, and for an end to egregious human rights abuses by the government and militant supporters of President Robert Mugabe.

> Godfrey, an MDC member granted asylum on September 7, 2007, received a letter from DHS informing him of DHS's intent to terminate his asylum status on June 2, 2009.[111] On June 12, 2009, President Obama met with MDC leader Morgan Tsvangirai at the White House, and expressed his "extraordinary admiration" for Tsvangirai's "courage and tenacity" in navigating "some very difficult political times in Zimbabwe." The U.S. State Department's annual human rights report for 2008 had spelled out those difficulties: "The government [of President Robert Mugabe

and the ruling ZANU-PF party] continued to engage in the pervasive and systematic abuse of human rights, which increased during the year. . . By year's end over 193 citizens had been killed in political violence that targeted members of the opposition party [i.e. the MDC]."

The letter Godfrey received from the Asylum Office did not explain why exactly DHS believed that membership in the MDC poses any kind of "terrorism"-related concern, stating only: "According to reliable sources, MDC members have engaged in violent retaliatory activities against ZANU members. Such activities may indicate inadmissibility grounds according to Sec. 212(a)(3)(B) of the INA." The letter informed Godfrey that in order to give him "the opportunity to respond to this adverse information" the asylum office had "scheduled a termination interview at least thirty (30) days after the date of this notice in order to give you sufficient time to prepare for the interview." It was unclear how an asylee in Godfrey's situation was expected to "respond" to "adverse information" without knowing what that information was. Other letters referring to other groups were similarly uninformative, e.g.: "According to reliable international sources, AAPO [All-Amhara Peoples' Organization] members have conspired and planned violent attacks against the government of Ethiopia."[112] Godfrey, the Zimbabwean asylee, and his lawyer attended his "termination interview"— and saw his asylum status confirmed, rather than terminated—without ever getting a clear explanation of what this was all about.

USCIS has since indicated that it is reviewing its decision to treat the MDC as a "Tier III" group. This is a welcome correction. But the termination scare, aside from throwing a group of blameless asylees into unnecessary panic, also raises the question how any branch of the U.S. government could have concluded that it was appropriate to treat the MDC—a group whose members have been on the receiving end of political violence in Zimbabwe for many years—as a "terrorist organization." While USCIS has repeatedly promised that it is resolving this problem with respect to the MDC, the fact that this happened, and continues to happen to other groups, is an indication of the inherent problems with the "Tier III" definition itself.

Still No Solution for Former Child Soldiers

"There is a clear legal prohibition on recruiting and using child soldiers, and yet around the world hundreds of thousands of boys and girls are used as combatants, porters, human mine detectors and sex slaves. While most serve in rebel or paramilitary groups, some government forces use child soldiers as well. In countries like Burma, Uganda, and Colombia, children's health and lives are endangered and their childhoods are sacrificed. . .

We must work to eliminate the use of child soldiers, but as long as the practice persists, we must also ensure that the law facilitates and encourages the rehabilitation and reintegration of these young people back into civilian life.

Sometimes the law contributes to the stigmatization of former child soldiers. For example, provisions of our immigration law brand former child soldiers as terrorists and prevent them from obtaining asylum or refugee status in the U.S. We must give the government flexibility to consider the unique mitigating circumstances facing child soldiers and allow child soldiers to raise such claims when they seek safe haven in our country."

Sen. Richard J. Durbin, April 24, 2007[113]

The plight of children used in armed conflict has been a focus of global advocacy and of Congressional attention in recent years. The Child Soldier Accountability Act of 2008, adopted unanimously by the House and the Senate, and signed into law by President Bush in October 2008, makes persons who knowingly recruit or use child soldiers subject to criminal prosecution under U.S. law if the perpetrators are on U.S. soil, and also provides for perpetrators of this crime to be denied entry to the United States or deported if already here.[114] The Child Soldier Prevention Act of 2008, legislation introduced by Senators Durbin and Brownback, passed unanimously by the the Senate and the House and signed into law by President Bush in December 2008, restricts U.S. military assistance to countries that use child soldiers in their national armies, or that support militia or paramilitary forces

that do so.[115] In acting to protect children from being used in armed conflict, and to hold perpetrators of that abuse accountable, Senators also expressed concern at the unwarranted exclusion of former child soldiers from refugee protection in the United States.[116]

But despite this concern for victims of child recruitment, and despite national and international efforts to target the *perpetrators* of those abuses, former child soldiers who seek asylum in the United States—or who were previously granted refugee protection here and now seek lawful permanent residence—continue to be barred under the immigration law's "terrorism"-related provisions and have been left out of the government's implementation of its discretionary authority to waive application of those same laws.

While the Department of Homeland Security is now implementing waivers for persons forced to give "material support" under duress whose cases are pending before DHS, there has been no implementation of waiver authority for applicants who were forced to engage in combat or who received "military-type training" against their wills. In addition, and as described below, the process for adjudicating any waiver of the "terrorism bars" in cases before the immigration courts is dysfunctional and inadequate, and does not even ensure that cases for which waivers have not yet been implemented are protected against deportation until such implementation can happen.

These gaps leave asylum applicants like Martine, the Congolese girl forcibly conscripted by armed rebels at age 12 who went on to advocate against the use of child soldiers, without relief. Martine, whose case is described in Part 4 of this report, has worked to draw attention to, and advocated for the prosecution of military commanders for, the sexual abuse of girls, and formerly worked with other former girl soldiers coping with the particular stigma and other challenges they face in reintegrating into their communities. These are the same causes the United States has supported through legislation. Yet even as that legislation has been enacted, Martine's application for asylum has been placed on hold, where it remains to this day.

The same has happened to the application for permanent residence of Lino Nakwa, the young man from South Sudan whose case was also described earlier in Part 4 of this report, who was forcibly subjected to what DHS has characterized as "military-type training" after being abducted by a South Sudanese rebel group. Human Rights First is aware of several other cases of refugees and asylees whose applications for permanent residence are still on hold because they were involved in armed conflicts as children, as long as 20 or 30 years ago in some cases.[117]

Still No Relief for Applicants in Immigration Court Proceedings

"How long, please?"

> Refugee from Sri Lanka, still waiting for a waiver after over four and a half years in removal proceedings

On October 23, 2008, DHS finally announced a process for implementing its discretionary authority to grant exemptions from the "terrorism bars" in immigration court removal cases. It had taken over three years from the time that waiver authority was enacted for this process to be implemented by DHS's sub-agencies, Immigration & Customs Enforcement (ICE) and U.S. Citizenship & Immigration Services (USCIS), in coordination with the Justice Department's Executive Office for Immigration Review. DHS stated that this process had taken effect on September 8, 2008, although DHS did not make the fact public until a month and a half later. (A copy of the U.S. Citizenship & Immigration Services fact sheet announcing and describing this process appears at Appendix D to this report.)

But the process announced a year ago only applies to a limited number of asylum seekers and other non-citizens currently on the road to deportation, and has proved surprisingly dysfunctional even for those who should theoretically be benefiting from it. As of September 2009, one year after the process went into effect, DHS had only considered seven immigration court cases for waivers nationwide, granting waivers to five of them.[118] Four of those

five cases involved applicants for asylum associated with the 10 named groups removed from the "Tier III" definition by the passage of the Consolidated Appropriations Act of 2008.[119]

No Waiver Without a Final Deportation Order— Years of Delay

One of several serious problems with the process for extending waivers to applicants in immigration court proceedings is that it only allows a person to be considered for a waiver once he or she has gone all the way through the immigration court process and any administrative appeals, and is subject to an order of removal that is administratively final. It also requires that the person have been found to be eligible for asylum (or whatever relief from removal the person was seeking) but for the "terrorism bars." DHS's protracted delays in announcing this process meant that for a long time, immigration judges who were issuing decisions in cases where they believed the "terrorism"-related bars applied were not necessarily making explicit findings as to how they would resolve the case if the "terrorism bars" were not an issue. In addition, when immigration judges *grant* asylum to applicants, they generally do not reach decisions on other forms of relief the person may have applied for, including protection under the Convention Against Torture, typically the only form of protection against removal that an asylum applicant might be eligible for if the "terrorism bars" were found to apply. If DHS Immigration & Customs Enforcement chooses to appeal on the issue of applicability of a "terrorism bar," and wins, cases then need to be sent back down to the immigration court for consideration of Convention Against Torture protection. The result is that applicants seeking to have their cases considered under this process face an interminable series of appeals and remands.

In cases Human Rights First has been following closely, it has generally taken asylum applicants in immigration court proceedings at least two years, and often longer, to receive an order from the Board of Immigration Appeals or from an immigration judge that will be considered a "final order" allowing their cases to be considered for a waiver. Applicants can then face additional delays of several months in receiving a decision on that waiver. And once they have been granted a waiver, they face further delay as they and ICE must make a motion to the immigration court to reopen their cases in order for them finally to be granted asylum. Consider the timelines of Kumar, the Sri Lankan fisherman, and B.T., the Nepalese medical worker, two of only seven cases nationwide to have been referred by Immigration & Customs Enforcement to U.S. Citizenship & Immigration services for waiver consideration as of September 2009:

B.T.

October 2005
Immigration judge grants B.T. asylum and withholding of removal, over DHS ICE objections that his having provided emergency medical care to wounded people, at gunpoint and at the behest of Maoist rebels who had abducted him, constituted "material support" to the Maoists. Because he was granting B.T. asylum and withholding of removal, the judge did not also decide whether B.T. was eligible for protection under the Convention Against Torture.[120]

November 2005
DHS ICE appeals.

September 2008
BIA grants DHS's appeal and denies B.T. asylum and withholding of removal based on the "material support" bar, but remands his case for the immigration judge to consider his eligibility for "deferral of removal" under the Convention Against Torture.

April 2009
Immigration judge rules that B.T. is indeed prohibited from being removed to Nepal under the Convention Against Torture, a prohibition that is not subject to any exceptions. Immigration judge enters a final order of removal against B.T., in accordance with Justice Department rules that require a person to be ordered deported in order to be granted either "withholding" or "deferral" of that order. B.T. finally has a final order of removal, and his attorney immediately writes to the DHS officials charged with administering the waiver process to alert them to this fact.

June 2009
USCIS indicates that it has not received B.T.'s file from ICE. The file was finally forwarded to USCIS later in the summer of 2009.

August 2009
B.T. is informed that he has been granted a waiver of the "material support" bar. He waits for his file to be returned to ICE for preparation of a joint motion to reopen his case.

October 2009
B.T.'s file finally returns to ICE. His attorney and ICE's counsel file a joint motion to the immigration court to reopen B.T.'s case so that he can finally be granted asylum.

Late October 2009
Four years to the day after he was first granted asylum and withholding of removal by an immigration judge, B.T. receives notice that he has been granted asylum and withholding of removal again.

Kumar

April 2005
Immigration judge denies Kumar asylum on the grounds that the ransom he had paid for his release from the LTTE rebels who had kidnapped him constituted "material support" to the LTTE. The Immigration Judge does not make explicit findings as to whether or not Kumar is otherwise eligible for asylum. Kumar is detained throughout his immigration court hearings.

May 2005
Kumar appeals the judge's decision to the Board of Immigration Appeals (BIA). Kumar is still detained.

May 2007
Kumar requests a waiver of the material support bar from the Secretary of Homeland Security, based on undisputed facts that he is likely to be persecuted by the Tamil Tigers and the Sri Lankan government.

July 2007
BIA denies Kumar's appeal on the material support issue, but remands to the Immigration Judge for findings as to his eligibility for asylum if material support were not an issue. Kumar is finally released from detention in July 2007, but only after he files a *habeas* petition in federal district court.

April 2008
Immigration Judge finds Kumar to be eligible for asylum but for the material support bar. DHS ICE, unexpectedly, appeals that decision to the BIA.

May 2009
BIA dismisses ICE's appeal. Kumar is now—finally—in a position to be considered for a waiver. His attorney writes to USCIS to ask for speedy processing. ICE then files a motion for reconsideration asking the BIA to rephrase one sentence of its decision that ICE considers ambiguous, even though ICE and Kumar are in agreement as to what the BIA meant.

June 2009
Over a month after the BIA issued its decision, USCIS indicates that it still has not received Kumar's file from Immigration & Customs Enforcement in order to consider his case for a waiver.

Summer 2009
USCIS finally receives the file, but concludes that it cannot consider Kumar's case for a waiver because Immigration & Customs Enforcement has filed a motion for reconsideration of the BIA decision.[121]

November 2009
Kumar still has not received a decision on a waiver.

The fact that a person must have received an administratively final order of removal in order to be considered for a waiver under DHS's process also means that even in cases where the applicant's eligibility for relief from removal is undisputed—but for the terrorism bar—there is no mechanism to allow that issue to be resolved except through completion of the full administrative appeals process. (Applicants in this situation have little reason to waive appeal, given the uncertainties of the waiver process.)

It also means that in order not to be deported while waiver consideration is underway, a person who has a final administrative order of removal must apply for a stay of removal from DHS. When and if a waiver is granted, DHS then needs to file a motion to reopen the person's removal case in order for the person actually to be granted asylum (or whatever form of relief he or she had applied for). If the final order of removal was issued by the Board of Immigration Appeals rather than the immigration court, this means, in practical terms, filing a motion to reopen to the BIA, only to have the BIA remand the case to the immigration court to confirm that security and background checks are complete. Human Rights First's experience of immigration court cases generally indicates that this last remand phase alone can result in delays of several months.[122]

No Waivers for the Unknown Number of Cases Denied Before September 8, 2008, Unless and Until the Applicant Gets Arrested

A second major limitation in DHS's waiver process for removal cases is that it applies only to cases where the final order of removal was entered on or after September 8, 2008. The only exception is where the applicant is detained, in which case the date of the final order does not matter. Neither DHS nor the Department of Justice, however, know how many people were ordered removed in a final fashion before September 8, 2008, after being barred from asylum or other forms of relief under the "terrorism"-related provisions of the immigration laws, because neither agency was tracking this information. As a result, the U.S. government cannot determine how many refugees may actually have been deported in violation of the Refugee Convention, nor make efforts to reverse outstanding deportation orders against legitimate refugees who might now be considered for waivers. DHS indicated in December 2008 that Immigration & Customs Enforcement had given up attempts to search its databases for such cases.[123]

No Protection Against Deportation Where DHS Has So Far Failed to Implement Waivers

Third, and perhaps most troubling, DHS's process only requires Immigration & Customs Enforcement to forward a case to U.S. Citizenship & Immigration Services for waiver consideration if the case falls within the scope of one of the exemption announcements already made by the Secretary of Homeland Security. This is a very significant problem, because, as explained earlier, the waiver announcements made to date leave out large categories of people who are eligible to be considered for waivers under the statutory discretionary authority that DHS, the Department of Justice, and the State Department say they are actively trying to implement.

Whereas applicants potentially eligible for waivers that have not yet been implemented whose cases are pending before the Department of Homeland Security are being placed on hold pending waiver implementation, identically situated applicants who are caught up in the removal process or actually have final orders of removal are not being considered for waivers at all. A large proportion of immigration court cases of which Human Rights First is aware where the terrorism-related bars are being invoked involve voluntary associations of one kind or another with alleged "Tier III" groups for which no waivers have been implemented, so that the failure to provide for waiver consideration in these cases has significant practical impact.

While some asylum applicants have been able to have their immigration cases adjourned repeatedly or held in abeyance ("administratively closed" is the immigration-court term) for some period of time pending DHS's implementation of its waiver authority, DHS ICE has actively opposed this solution in some cases. ICE recently argued to the immigration court, for example, that it should no longer delay the deportation case of an asylum applicant from Ethiopia whose peaceful political activities and limited humanitarian contributions ICE considers to be "material support" to a group it deems to be a "Tier III" organization. ICE's motion states its position: "[C]ases involving material support provided to [Tier III] terrorist organizations are on hold with USCIS. However, the ICE/OPLA directive is to move forward with cases such as the respondent's. As the respondent is not eligible for any of the exemptions in place at this time . . . there is no reason to continue this case indefinitely."[124]

Other asylum applicants are continuing to pursue their cases all the way through the removal process without knowing whether implementation of waivers that might resolve their "terrorism bar" issues will happen before they are actually deported—or, if it does, whether they will be able to benefit.

> A woman who applied for asylum from political persecution in Eritrea, for example, and whose testimony was found to be credible, was denied all relief by an immigration judge based on

the fact that she had provided support, in the late 1970's, to a group then fighting for Eritrea's independence from Ethiopia. Ethiopia at that time was ruled by the notoriously brutal Dergue regime, which jailed this woman and subjected her to repeated torture. Because he found that she was barred from asylum based on the "terrorism bars," the immigration judge did not decide whether the woman was otherwise statutorily eligible for refugee protection. The Board of Immigration Appeals agreed that the terrorism bars applied. This asylum applicant's appeal is currently pending before the federal court of appeals. If the court of appeals denies her appeal based on the "terrorism bars," this woman could be deported without ever having received a decision on the merits of her asylum claim and without ever having been considered for a waiver.[125]

The deep flaws in the waiver process for immigration court cases are particularly troubling because both the Board of Immigration Appeals and the Department of Homeland Security itself have at various times pointed to the existence of DHS's statutory waiver authority as the device that is to save the "terrorism"-related provisions of the immigration law from their unintended unjust consequences and from violation of U.S. treaty obligations not to return to persecution refugees who are entitled to protection under the Refugee Convention.[126] Asylum seekers in removal proceedings who are facing actual deportation implicate those obligations in a very immediate way, yet they are being neglected by the waiver process or left out of it altogether.

Unnecessary Detention Based on the "Terrorism Bars"

"I told them 'I want to apply for asylum' and they put me in this place. It's very terrible here . . . All the time I read the Bible, I'm working, I'm praying, but otherwise I'm still in jail."

> S.K., Chin asylum applicant from Burma, speaking in June 2006 from the immigration detention center where she had then been held for nearly two years[127]

Refugees who request asylum upon arriving at a U.S. airport or border are subject to mandatory detention under the immigration law's "expedited removal" provisions until they pass a preliminary screening interview with an asylum officer. While the law allows for asylum seekers who have passed those interviews to be released thereafter, many are not.[128]

Applicants in this situation who are considered to fall under one of the immigration law's "terrorism"-related provisions face long delays in litigating those issues, and the fact that DHS ICE has invoked a "terrorism bar" in their cases is often used as an additional reason to deny them release.

> A member of a Somali minority clan, Liban walked up to U.S. immigration officers at a California border crossing in August 2008 and told them that he was a refugee from Somalia. He was immediately detained, and has been held in a California immigration jail since that date. In his application for asylum and his testimony before the immigration court, Liban explained that he fled his country after armed militia men who belonged to the same majority clan his family had suffered under for many years ordered him to come fight with them. The men told him that they belonged to Al-Shabaab, a radical armed Islamist group that the United States later designated as a Tier I terrorist organization. When Liban objected, the armed men knocked him unconscious and then beat him severely. They took him to a house where they were already holding other prisoners, one of whom was a cousin of Liban's. The next day, their captors came and tried to hand Liban's cousin a gun. When the cousin refused to take it, they beat him, then shot him dead in front of Liban. The men beat Liban and told him that they would kill him, too, if he did not do what they said.

> After leaving Liban locked up for several hours with his cousin's body, the militiamen came back and put a gun in his hands. Liban had never held a gun in his life and had no idea if this one was loaded. His captors took him to the edge of the town. On their way, they passed a row of men holding guns who Liban assumed were Al-Shabaab fighters. Liban's captors led him down the road, ahead of where their fighters were posted, and told him to stand there and to hold his gun so that it was visible. That was the only instruction they gave him. Liban is not sure what the point of his presence there was, but guesses that the militiamen were using him as a human decoy, to be an easy target for enemy gunfire in the event of any fighting. He was able to escape after a little more than a day, during which there was no fighting and he never used the gun. After he escaped, his captors retaliated against his family, killing an uncle and threatening to kill the rest unless they revealed Liban's whereabouts.[129]

The immigration judge found Liban's testimony to be credible, that his case was corroborated, and that he was under duress when he stood in the road with the gun, but held that he was barred from asylum because his unwilling presence on an empty road constituted "material support" to Al-Shabaab. Liban is appealing this determination to the Board of Immigration Appeals, arguing that he committed no act of support to Al-Shabaab and has no idea whether his involuntary physical presence in that location even benefitted them in any way. Although the immigration judge explicitly noted that he deserved to be granted a waiver by DHS, under the procedures DHS has established for this, Liban's case will not be considered for such a waiver until his appeal is finally decided. Meanwhile, Liban, who has a cousin and multiple family friends in the United States who would be happy to take him in, faces indefinite detention, as DHS had previously denied his request for release.

In addition, DHS ICE has invoked mandatory detention in isolated immigration cases deemed to be subject to one of the overly broad "terrorism"-related bars. It is clearly not ICE's practice across the board to detain everyone who is in immigration court proceedings and whose case is affected by any of the overly broad "terrorism"-related bars. DHS Headquarters has also confirmed to Human Rights First that it is not DHS policy to detain all such applicants. In fact, DHS's process for granting "waivers" to people who have already received final orders of removal based on a "terrorism"-related ground explicitly contemplates different processes for detained and non-detained cases, which would make no sense if detention were systematic.[130] Nonetheless, local ICE offices continue to make this claim in individual cases, which appear to be selected for this treatment at random.

ICE earlier this year argued that a Salvadoran man with no criminal record, detained in Texas with his two young children, could not be released because he had been forced on one occasion to move boxes by the FMLN guerrilla group over 20 years ago in El Salvador. The FMLN has been a legal political party in El Salvador since 1992 and is now one of the two major political parties in the country, where it won the presidential elections held in March of this year. The immigration judge who conducted a custody hearing in this man's case ruled that the "material support" bar did not apply and ordered his release. Although ICE ultimately released him, ICE is still pursuing an appeal of the immigration judge's release order, arguing that this father of two is subject to mandatory detention based on what happened to him 20 years ago. ICE argues that the fact that he acted under duress is legally irrelevant.[131]

DHS ICE also invoked mandatory detention in the case of an asylum seeker and survivor of torture from Ethiopia who has been living in the United States for over six years and had previously been granted asylum by the immigration court.

> Mulatu is a middle-aged father of five children who arrived in the United States in 2003 and applied for asylum. A member of the Oromo ethnic group in Ethiopia, he testified that he had joined the Oromo Liberation Front (OLF) in 1991, when the OLF became part of the transitional government in Ethiopia after the fall of the Mengistu regime. During the period when the OLF was part of the transitional government, Mulatu chaired a local fundraising committee. He testified that after the OLF left the transitional government, there was conflict within the organization over the use of armed force, and that he continued as a simple member of the OLF after that time, supporting the peaceful faction within the party. Nevertheless, Ethiopian security forces arrested him on several occasions and tortured him. His family was threatened, Mulatu was fired from his job, and his siblings and friends were also arrested. The immigration court found his testimony to be credible and granted him asylum in 2006, just before the Board of Immigration Appeals (BIA) issued its decision in *Matter of S-K*, in which it held that any group that uses force against an established government should be considered a "Tier III terrorist organization." DHS Immigration & Customs Enforcement (ICE) appealed, arguing that Mulatu's association with the OLF barred him from refugee protection based on the Board's recent decision. In early 2008, the BIA reversed the immigration judge's decision on those grounds, and remanded the case back to the immigration court for reconsideration.

> In June 2009, Mulatu, who had now been living peacefully in the United States for six years, appeared before the immigration court for a new hearing. At the end of the hearing the immigration judge indicated that she would review the case and issue a decision at a later date. ICE arrested Mulatu immediately after the hearing, and he has been detained ever since. The immigration judge ultimately reversed her earlier decision based on the BIA's decision in *Matter of S-K-*, but held that Mulatu was entitled to protection under the Convention Against Torture based on the fact that he had been subjected to torture in

Ethiopia in the past and would likely be tortured again if returned there. As Mulatu then appealed the denial of asylum to the BIA, he remained in jail, even though many refugees with indistinguishable political histories are pursuing their asylum claims before the immigration courts in freedom or are living in the United States as asylees, permanent residents, or U.S. citizens.

On October 27, 2009, the BIA denied Mulatu's appeal on the "material support" issue, but affirmed all the aspects of the immigration judge's decision that were in his favor.[132] Although he was found to be eligible for asylum but for the "terrorism bars" and was found to face a probability of torture in Ethiopia, he is not being considered for a waiver because DHS has not yet implemented its authority to grant waivers to people who had voluntary associations with "Tier III" groups. He remains detained in immigration custody.

The Human Cost

Eight years after the passage of the USA PATRIOT Act, legitimate refugees continue to bear the brunt of immigration laws intended to keep out terrorists. As the inability of the relevant federal agencies to resolve that situation through the implementation of discretionary "waiver" authority has now entered its fourth year, the law's impact on asylum seekers and refugees in the United States continues to grow. Refugees whose petitions to be reunited with their families have been on hold for several years no longer know what to tell their spouses or their children who are growing up without them. Asylum seekers who are detained continue to suffer in jail-like surroundings while their cases wend their way through the protracted administrative appeals process that they must complete before DHS ICE's extreme interpretations of the "terrorism bars" are dismissed, or the asylum seekers themselves are ordered deported and can for the first time be considered for a "waiver" of those bars. Asylum seekers, and refugees and asylees already granted protection—years ago in many cases—see their prospects for integration into the United States delayed indefinitely because their requests for asylum or for permanent residence are blocked by the immigration law's sweeping "terrorism"-related provisions.

Separating Families

In a number of cases that Human Rights First has been monitoring, delays resulting from the immigration law's "terrorism bars" have prolonged refugees' separation from their spouses and children for periods of up to four years. Many asylum seekers are unable to take their spouses and children with them when they flee their countries. Being granted asylum allows them to petition for reunification with these family members, who typically have no other way of gaining admission to the United States. People already granted asylum or refugee status are suffering the same effects, as their petitions for family reunification have also been put on hold. Unlike other immigrants with lawful status in the United States, refugees and asylees who are here because of threats to their safety back home do not have the option of visiting their families in their home countries while their petitions to bring them here are pending. Human Rights First regularly hears asylum seekers and asylees whose petitions for family reunification are on hold due to the "terrorism bars" express the fear that something bad will happen to their families before their petitions are processed; that their families will feel abandoned; that their young children will no longer remember them.

For one torture survivor whose petitions for her children have been pending for nearly three years based on the immigration law's "Tier III" definition, resolution, when it comes, will have come too late:

> Rachel was granted asylum in the United States based on persecution she had suffered as a result of her peaceful activism for the rights of Cameroon's English-speaking minority. This persecution included torture that left her with scars all over her body. After Rachel was granted asylum, she filed a petition to bring her children to the United States. The Department of Homeland Security placed her petition for family reunification on hold on the theory that the Southern Cameroons National Council (SCNC), the Anglophone independence movement to which Rachel belonged, while not itself involved in violence, was associated with another group, the Southern Cameroons Youth Council (SCYL), that the Department of Homeland Security believed had engaged in violent acts. Rachel's petitions for her children have been pending for close to three years. Representatives of the Department of Homeland Security recently

indicated that they were reconsidering their assessment of the SCNC and indeed of the SCYL.[133] But in the meantime, one of Rachel's children has died of natural causes.[134]

Other applicants worry about the safety of family members living at risk in exile or in some cases being threatened in their absence by the same forces who had previously targeted them:

> Tashi fled Nepal in late 2006 to escape threats from Maoist militants. Upon arriving in the United States, Tashi applied for asylum, which was promptly granted. He then, in early 2007, filed petitions for his wife and two little children, and waited anxiously for them to be approved. When he received no decision for months beyond the normal processing times, Tashi made repeated fruitless inquiries to U.S. Citizenship & Immigration Services. After writing to the USCIS Ombudsman, he finally received a response: "These cases are on hold because it appears that you and your family members are on hold under Section 212(a)(3)(B) of the INA, and USCIS currently has no authority not to apply the inadmissibility ground(s) to which you and your family members appear to be subject."
>
> When Tashi, who had been handling all of his immigration applications himself without legal assistance, searched the internet for section 212(a)(3)(B) of the Immigration & Nationality Act and read it, he was shocked. "To the best of my knowledge," he said, "I have never ever in my life done anything that would even in the minutest way morally or materially support any act of terrorism. In fact I had to flee my country and seek asylum here because of all sorts of threats I received from Maoists (who I understand are listed in one of the terrorist categories of the U.S. government) for doing just the opposite: not agreeing to support them monetarily and morally in their violent activities and ideology." It appears that the reason Tashi's petitions were on hold was his support for the *Nepali Congress Party,* which the Department of Homeland Security was characterizing as a "Tier III terrorist organization," to general confusion. "This is the party accused by other political parties of being too inclined towards the western democracies or of being agents of America, Britain, or even India," Tashi notes. The Department of Homeland Security's conclusion that the Nepali Congress Party should be considered a "Tier III" group appears to have stemmed from activities of the group during the 1960's. Tashi first became involved in the party in 1991. While his petitions for family reunification were held up by historical error,

Tashi's wife received further threatening phone calls, and has had to move with the children for their safety.[135]

Tashi's petitions to be reunited with his wife and children were finally approved on November 2, 2009, after the Department of Homeland Security recognized that it had mischaracterized the Nepali Congress Party as a "Tier III" group, at least with respect to the period of Tashi's involvement. After close to three years of unnecessary separation and anxiety, Tashi is looking forward to welcoming his wife and little children, "one of whom," he says, "hadn't even walked her first steps or mumbled her first words when I left Nepal." But asylees and refugees associated with other groups DHS has considered to be "Tier IIII" organizations are still waiting, with no indication of when they may see their families again.

Applicants in immigration court cases for whom family separation is an urgent issue face the same problem. Kumar, the Sri Lankan refugee whose case was described earlier, has been waiting for four years for his case to be resolved as his country has been wracked by civil war and its immediate aftermath. He remains unable to do anything to extract his wife from that situation until he is granted asylum.

Prolonging Detention

The "terrorism bars" have a particularly devastating effect on applicants for asylum who are detained by Immigration & Customs Enforcement (ICE). Applicants in this situation have faced detention for two years or more as their cases go through an endless process of administrative adjudication. These have included cases where both the immigration court and the Board of Immigration Appeals indicated the hope or expectation that the applicants' problems would be resolved through the grant of a waiver by the Department of Homeland Security.

One of the first such cases was that of S-K-, the Burmese Chin woman who was denied asylum by an immigration judge in 2005 and by the Board of Immigration Appeals in 2006 because she had provided "material support" to the Chin National Front (CNF). While S-K- was ultimately granted asylum after a legislative amendment in 2007 removed the

CNF and nine other groups from the scope of the immigration law's "Tier III definition," she spent over two years in an immigration jail in Texas while her case made its way through the administrative appeals process, before DHS Immigration & Customs Enforcement finally released her in late August 2006. More than three years after S-K-'s case was concluded, other applicants unjustly affected by the "terrorism" bars continue to face prolonged detention.

Two years after his release from the jail-like detention center where he spent the first two and a half years of his time in the United States, and over five months after a final administrative order found him to be eligible for asylum but for his ransom payment, Kumar, the Sri Lankan asylum seeker, is still forced to wear a large, uncomfortable, and humiliating electronic monitoring device on his ankle. Despite repeated requests by Kumar's lawyer, DHS has refused to remove this electronic device.

Liban, the young man from Somalia profiled earlier, has been detained since August of 2008. Louis, the asylum seeker from Burundi who was ultimately granted asylum after the Board of Immigration Appeals rejected ICE's claim that being robbed of one's lunch and four dollars by armed rebels constitutes "material support to a terrorist organization," was detained for over 20 months. Mulatu, the Oromo citizen of Ethiopia whose case was described earlier, has been detained since June 2009 and remains in jail even though the Board of Immigration Appeals just affirmed his entitlement to protection under the Convention Against Torture.

Delaying Integration

For asylum seekers, prolonged delays in processing their applications for asylum due to the "terrorism" bars can pose a threat to their ability to house and feed themselves. The asylum regulations only allow asylum seekers to apply for permission to work once their applications for asylum have been pending for 150 days without being denied by an immigration judge. Human Rights First has provided legal assistance to a number of asylum seekers who have been reduced to extreme poverty and/or homelessness due to delays in processing their applications for asylum.

A lack of lasting immigration status also makes asylum seekers ineligible for the financial aid that many of them need in order to be able to resume educations interrupted by persecution and flight. Being able to work and pursue an education and a career helps asylum seekers regain the control over their lives that they lost when they became refugees. For those who have dependents, being unable to work or to plan for the future for an extended period makes it extremely difficult for them to support their families, who are often stranded in unstable or unsafe situations abroad, or to prepare for their arrival.

For asylees and refugees, who have already been granted protection, permanent residence has significant legal and practical benefits. Certain jobs and professional licenses require permanent residence. Permanent residence, and to a greater extent U.S. citizenship, for which five years of permanent residence is generally a prerequisite, also allows asylees and refugees to file immigrant visa petitions for members of their family not covered by the asylee/refugee family reunification process. Permanent residence also puts asylees and refugees, who by definition have lost the protection of their country of nationality, on the path to U.S. citizenship. Many asylees and refugees who have never had the opportunity to vote in a free election in their own country look forward to becoming U.S. citizens so as to be able to take part fully in the civic life of the United States.

Asylees and refugees often need to travel abroad to visit family members in exile in third countries who cannot obtain visas to visit their relatives in the United States. A number of asylees and refugees whose stalled applications for permanent residence Human Rights First has been monitoring have jobs that require international travel, or have had to decline business opportunities that would require them to leave the country. International travel for non-U.S. citizens resident in the United States is significantly easier if they hold permanent residence, as a number of countries will waive visa requirements for people in this situation. Asylees and refugees who know that they have been deemed to be inadmissible to the United States on "terrorism"-related grounds are often afraid to travel outside the United States while their situations remain unresolved, for fear of not being allowed back in or detained upon return.

Many asylees and refugees are unaware that their applications for permanent residence are on hold based on the "terrorism"-related provisions of the immigration law, and when they are able to obtain this information, the way it is conveyed is uninformative and frightening. Human Rights First is regularly contacted by refugees and asylees who, having learned for the first time that their cases are on hold based on "212(a)(3)(B) of the INA," have just searched for this subsection of the law on the Internet and are taken aback at the results:

> Photoson was admitted to the United States as a refugee from Liberia in 1998. His application for permanent residence has been on hold for nearly three years, and he had no idea why. This was not for lack of inquiring. After several communications with USCIS yielded no substantive responses, in June of 2009, Photoson received a form letter in response to his most recent inquiry about the status of his case. The letter stated: "Your case is on hold because you appear to be inadmissible under 212(a)(3)(B) of the INA, and USCIS currently has no authority not to apply the inadmissibility ground(s) to which you appear to be subject."[136]

> Left to figure out on his own what this might mean, Photoson looked up section 212(a)(3)(B) of the Immigration & Nationality Act. He was shocked at what he found. "What it boils down to," he told Human Rights First, "is that they think I am a terrorist, or that I have engaged in terrorist activities, or that I am likely to engage in such acts in the future." Photoson is confused and indignant. He was never a member of any of the rebel armies that destroyed his country—quite the opposite, he fled Liberia to escape their violence. "My friends and I went to Catholic school," he says, "we believed in the sanctity of human life." He recalls that he loved the United States before he ever came here; it was the focus of his dreams during the years he spent in a refugee camp in West Africa. He has been living in the U.S. for nearly 12 years. His two youngest children, now 11 and 6 years of age, are U.S. citizens. For seven years he worked as a field service engineer at a number of security-sensitive sites, including the U.S. Treasury, all assignments that required extensive criminal and background checks. "This country is the land that is flowing with milk and honey, that has given me so much," Photoson says. "What motive do I have to harm it?" He cannot

believe that U.S. immigration law has redefined him as a terrorist, and he would like to know how this happened.

Permanent residence has emotional value for asylees and refugees that goes beyond its immediate practical importance. It gives them the confidence that they are fully and permanently welcome in the United States, which is important for people who have suffered forced migration. It gives them an immigration status that everyone in this country recognizes. Although "green cards" have not been green in many years, most employers, acquaintances, and mortgage officers in the United States are familiar with permanent residence, and it is an immigration status that does not require potentially painful explanations of a past history of trauma. Conversely, being unable to obtain a "green card" after living and working *legally* in this country for many years, and with a form of status that makes a person eligible for permanent residence, is deeply demoralizing, and when the reason for this is an alleged ground of inadmissibility related to "terrorism," that state of affairs becomes a permanent source of anxiety for already vulnerable people.

Conclusion

The new leadership at the Departments of Homeland Security, Justice, and State, along with Congress, has the opportunity now to resolve this problem effectively. In order to do this, Congress and the Administration must fix the underlying statutory definitions and agency legal positions that gave rise to the problem. Specific recommendations for a comprehensive solution are outlined at the beginning of this report. These changes are critical to ensure that the United States can meet its obligations to protect legitimate refugees and to allow the agencies involved to focus their enforcement efforts on the people Congress intended the terrorism-related provisions of the immigration laws to target. Until this happens, the problems described in this report will persist.

7. Appendices

A. Relevant Statutory Provisions

Terrorism- and Security-related Inadmissibility Grounds
Immigration & Nationality Act (INA) Section 212(a)(3) (8 U.S.C. § 1182(a)(3))

(a) *Classes of Aliens Ineligible for Visas or Admission.*—Except as otherwise provided in this Act, aliens who are inadmissible under the following paragraphs are ineligible to receive visas and ineligible to be admitted to the United States:

....

(3) *Security and related grounds.*—

(A) In general.—Any alien who a consular officer or the Attorney General knows, or has reasonable ground to believe, seeks

to enter the United States to engage solely, principally, or incidentally in—

(i) any activity

(I) to violate any law of the United States relating to espionage or sabotage or

(II) to violate or evade any law prohibiting the export from the United States of goods, technology, or sensitive information,

(ii) any other unlawful activity, or

(iii) any activity a purpose of which is the opposition to, or the control or overthrow of, the Government of the United States by force, violence, or other unlawful means, is inadmissible.

(B) Terrorist activities.—

(i) IN GENERAL.—Any alien who—

(I) has engaged in a terrorist activity,

(II) a consular officer, the Attorney General, or the Secretary of Homeland Security knows, or has reasonable ground to believe, is engaged in or is likely to engage after entry in any terrorist activity (as defined in clause (iv));

(III) has, under circumstances indicating an intention to cause death or serious bodily harm, incited terrorist activity;

(IV) is a representative (as defined in clause (v)) of—

(aa) a terrorist organization (as defined in clause (vi)); or

(bb) a political, social, or other group that endorses or espouses terrorist activity;

(V) is a member of a terrorist organization described in subclause (I) or (II) of clause (vi);

(VI) is a member of a terrorist organization described in clause (vi)(III), unless the alien can demonstrate by clear and convincing evidence that the alien did not know, and should not reasonably have known, that the organization was a

terrorist organization;

(VII) endorses or espouses terrorist activity or persuades others to endorse or espouse terrorist activity or support a terrorist

organization;

(VIII) has received military-type training (as defined in section 2339D(c)(1) of title 18, United States Code) from or on

behalf of any organization that, at the time the training was received, was a terrorist organization (as defined in clause

(vi)); or

(IX) is the spouse or child of an alien who is inadmissible under this subparagraph, if the activity causing the alien to be

found inadmissible occurred within the last 5 years, is inadmissible.

(ii) EXCEPTION—Subclause (VII) of clause (i) does not apply to a spouse or child—

(I) who did not know or should not reasonably have known of the activity causing the alien to be found inadmissible

under this section; or

(II) whom the consular officer or Attorney General has reasonable grounds to believe has renounced the activity causing the alien to be found inadmissible under this section.

(iii) TERRORIST ACTIVITY DEFINED.—As used in this chapter, the term "terrorist activity" means any activity which is unlawful under the laws of the place where it is committed (or which, if it had been committed in the United States, would be unlawful under the laws of the United States or any State) and which involves any of the following:

(I) The highjacking or sabotage of any conveyance (including an aircraft, vessel, or vehicle).

(II) The seizing or detaining, and threatening to kill, injure, or continue to detain, another individual in order to compel a third person (including a governmental organization) to do or abstain from doing any act as an explicit or implicit condition for the release of the individual seized or detained.

(III) A violent attack upon an internationally protected person (as defined in section 1116(b)(4) of title 18, United States Code) or upon the liberty of such a person.

(IV) An assassination.

(V) The use of any—

(a) biological agent, chemical agent, or nuclear weapon or device, or

(b) explosive, firearm, or other weapon or dangerous device (other than for mere personal monetary gain), with intent to endanger, directly or indirectly, the safety of one or more individuals or to cause substantial damage to property.

(VI) A threat, attempt, or conspiracy to do any of the foregoing.

(iv) ENGAGE IN TERRORIST ACTIVITY DEFINED.—As used in this chapter, the term "engage in terrorist activity" means, in an individual capacity or as a member of an organization—

(I) to commit or to incite to commit, under circumstances indicating an intention to cause death or serious bodily injury, a terrorist activity;

(II) to prepare or plan a terrorist activity;

(III) to gather information on potential targets for terrorist activity;

(IV) to solicit funds or other things of value for—

(aa) a terrorist activity;

(bb) a terrorist organization described in clause (vi)(I) or (vi)(II); or

(cc) a terrorist organization described in clause (vi)(III), unless the solicitor can demonstrate by clear and convincing evidence that he did not know, and should not reasonably have known, that the organization was a terrorist organization;

(V) to solicit any individual—

(aa) to engage in conduct otherwise described in this subsection;

(bb) for membership in a terrorist organization described in clause (vi)(I) or (vi)(II); or

(cc) for membership in a terrorist organization described in clause (vi)(III) unless the solicitor can demonstrate by clear and convincing evidence that he did not know, and should not reasonably have known, that the organization was a terrorist organization; or

(VI) to commit an act that the actor knows, or reasonably should know, affords material support, including a safe house, transportation, communications, funds, transfer of funds or other material financial benefit, false documentation or identification, weapons (including chemical, biological, or radiological weapons), explosives, or training—

(aa) for the commission of a terrorist activity;

(bb) to any individual who the actor knows, or reasonably should know, has committed or plans to commit a terrorist activity;

(cc) to a terrorist organization described in subclause (I) or (II) of clause (vi) or to any member of such an organization; or

(dd) to a terrorist organization described in clause (vi)(III), or to any member of such an organization, unless the actor can demonstrate by clear and convincing evidence that the actor did not know, and should not reasonably have known, that the organization was a terrorist organization.

(v) REPRESENTATIVE DEFINED.—As used in this paragraph, the term "representative" includes an officer, official, or

spokesman of an organization, and any person who directs, counsels, commands, or induces an organization or its members to engage in terrorist activity.

(vi) TERRORIST ORGANIZATION DEFINED.—As used in clause (i)(VI) and clause (iv), the term 'terrorist organization' means an organization—

(I) designated under section 219;

(II) otherwise designated, upon publication in the Federal Register, by the Secretary of State in consultation with or upon

the request of the Attorney General or the Secretary of Homeland Security, as a terrorist organization, after finding that the

organization engages in the activities described in subclauses (I) through (VI) of clause (iv); or

(III) that is a group of two or more individuals, whether organized or not, which engages in, or has a subgroup which

engages in, the activities described in subclauses (I) through (VI) of clause (iv).

Statutory Waiver Authority
INA Section 212(d)(3)(B)(i) (8 U.S.C. § 1182(d)(3)(B)(i))

(d) Temporary Admission of Nonimmigrants.—

....

(3)(B) (i) The Secretary of State, after consultation with the Attorney General and the Secretary of Homeland Security, or the Secretary of Homeland Security, after consultation with the Secretary of State and the Attorney General, may determine in such Secretary's sole unreviewable discretion that subsection (a)(3)(B) shall not apply with respect to an alien within the scope of that subsection or that subsection (a)(3)(B)(vi)(III) shall not apply to a group within the scope of that subsection, except that no such waiver may be extended to an alien who is within the scope of subsection (a)(3)(B)(i)(II), no such waiver may be extended to an alien who is a member or representative of, has voluntarily and knowingly engaged in or endorsed or espoused or persuaded others to endorse or espouse or support terrorist activity on behalf of, or has voluntarily and knowingly received military-type training from a terrorist organization that is described in subclause (I) or (II) of subsection (a)(3)(B)(vi), and no such waiver may be extended to a group that has engaged terrorist activity against the United States or another democratic country or that has purposefully engaged in a pattern or practice of terrorist activity that is directed at civilians. Such a determination shall neither prejudice the ability of the United States Government to commence criminal or civil proceedings involving a beneficiary of such a determination or any other person, nor create any substantive or procedural right or benefit for a beneficiary of such a determination or any other person. Notwithstanding any other provision of law (statutory or nonstatutory), including section 2241 of title 28, or any other habeas corpus provision, and sections 1361 and 1651 of such title, no court shall have jurisdiction to review such a determination or revocation except in a proceeding for review of a final order of removal pursuant to section 1252 of this title, and review shall be limited to the extent provided in section 1252 (a)(2)(D). The Secretary of State may not exercise the discretion provided in this clause with respect to an alien at any time during which the alien is the subject of pending removal proceedings under section 1229a of this title.

(ii) Not later than 90 days after the end of each fiscal year, the Secretary of State and the Secretary of Homeland Security shall each provide to the Committees on the Judiciary of the House of Representatives and of the Senate, the Committee on International Relations of the House of Representatives, the Committee on Foreign Relations of the Senate, and the Committee on Homeland Security of the House of Representatives a report on the aliens to whom such Secretary has applied clause (i). Within one week of applying clause (i) to a group, the Secretary of State or the Secretary of Homeland Security shall provide a report to such Committees.

Bars to Asylum
INA Section 208(b)(2)(A) (8 U.S.C. § 1158(b)(2)(A))

(2) *Exceptions.*—

(A) In general.—Paragraph (1) [the provisions allowing for a grant of asylum] shall not apply to an alien if the Attorney General determines that—

(i)   en ordered, incited, assisted, or otherwise participated in the persecution of any person on account of race, religion, nationality, membership in a particular social group, or political opinion;

(ii) the alien, having been convicted by a final judgment of a particularly serious crime, constitutes a danger to the community of the United States;

(iii) there are serious reasons for believing that the alien has committed a nonpolitical crime outside the United States prior to the arrival of the alien in the United States;

(iv) there are reasonable grounds for regarding the alien as a danger to the security of the United States;

(v)　the alien is described in subclause (I), (II), (III), (IV), or (VI) of section 212(a)(3)(B)(i) or section 237(a)(4)(B) (relating to terrorist activity), unless, in the case only of an alien described in subclause (IV) of section 212(a)(3)(B)(i), the Attorney General determines, in the Attorney General's discretion, that there are not reasonable grounds for regarding the alien as a danger to the security of the United States; or

(vi)　the alien was firmly resettled in another country prior to arriving in the United States.

(B) Special rules.—

(i)　Conviction of aggravated felony.— For purposes of clause (ii) of subparagraph (A), an alien who has been convicted of an aggravated felony shall be considered to have been convicted of a particularly serious crime.

(ii)　Offenses.— The Attorney General may designate by regulation offenses that will be considered to be a crime described in clause (ii) or (iii) of subparagraph (A).

*(C) Additional limitations.—*The Attorney General may by regulation establish additional limitations and conditions, consistent with this section, under which an alien shall be ineligible for asylum under paragraph (1).

*(D) No judicial review.—*There shall be no judicial review of a determination of the Attorney General under subparagraph (A)(v).

Bars to Withholding of Removal
INA Section 241(b)(3)(B) (8 U.S.C. § 1231(b)(3)(B))

(B)　*Exception.—*Subparagraph (A) [prohibiting the removal of any person to a country where his or her life or freedom would be threatened on account of his or her race, religion, nationality, membership in a particular social group, or political opinion] does not apply to an alien deportable under section 237(a)(4)(D) or if the Attorney General decides that—

i.　the alien ordered, incited, assisted, or otherwise participated in the persecution of an individual because of the individual's race, religion, nationality, membership in a particular social group, or political opinion;

ii.　the alien, having been convicted by a final judgment of a particularly serious crime, is a danger to the community of the United States;

iii.　there are serious reasons to believe that the alien committed a serious nonpolitical crime outside the United States before the alien arrived in the United States; or

iv.　there are reasonable grounds to believe that the alien is a danger to the security of the United States.

For purposes of clause (ii), an alien who has been convicted of an aggravated felony (or felonies) for which the alien has been sentenced to an aggregate term of imprisonment of at least 5 years shall be considered to have committed a particularly serious crime. The previous sentence shall not preclude the Attorney General from determining that, notwithstanding the length of sentence imposed, an alien has been convicted of a particularly serious crime. For purposes of clause (iv), an alien who is described in section 237(a)(4)(B) shall be considered to be an alien with respect to whom there are reasonable grounds for regarding as a danger to the security of the United States.

General Grounds of Inadmissibility under the Immigration & Nationality Act
INA Section 212(a) (8 U.S.C. § 11182(a))

(a) Classes of aliens ineligible for visas or admission

Except as otherwise provided in this chapter, aliens who are inadmissible under the following paragraphs are ineligible to receive visas and ineligible to be admitted to the United States:

(1) Health-related grounds

(A) In general.— Any alien—

(i) who is determined (in accordance with regulations prescribed by the Secretary of Health and Human Services) to have a communicable disease of public health significance;

(ii) except as provided in subparagraph (C), who seeks admission as an immigrant, or who seeks adjustment of status to the status of an alien lawfully admitted for permanent residence, and who has failed to present documentation of having received vaccination against vaccine-preventable diseases, which shall include at least the following diseases: mumps, measles, rubella, polio, tetanus and diphtheria toxoids, pertussis, influenza type B and hepatitis B, and any other vaccinations against vaccine-preventable diseases recommended by the Advisory Committee for Immunization Practices,

(iii) who is determined (in accordance with regulations prescribed by the Secretary of Health and Human Services in consultation with the Attorney General)—

(I) to have a physical or mental disorder and behavior associated with the disorder that may pose, or has posed, a threat to the property, safety, or welfare of the alien or others, or

(II) to have had a physical or mental disorder and a history of behavior associated with the disorder, which behavior has posed a threat to the property, safety, or welfare of the alien or others and which behavior is likely to recur or to lead to other harmful behavior, or

(iv) who is determined (in accordance with regulations prescribed by the Secretary of Health and Human Services) to be a drug abuser or addict,

is inadmissible.

(B) Waiver authorized.— For provision authorizing waiver of certain clauses of subparagraph (A), see subsection (g) of this section.

(C) Exception from immunization requirement for adopted children 10 years of age or younger.— Clause (ii) of subparagraph (A) shall not apply to a child who—

(i) is 10 years of age or younger,

(ii) is described in section 1101 (b)(1)(F) of this title, and

(iii) is seeking an immigrant visa as an immediate relative under section 1151 (b) of this title,

if, prior to the admission of the child, an adoptive parent or prospective adoptive parent of the child, who has sponsored the child for admission as an immediate relative, has executed an affidavit stating that the parent is aware of the provisions of subparagraph (A)(ii) and will ensure that, within 30 days of the child's admission, or at the earliest time that is medically appropriate, the child will receive the vaccinations identified in such subparagraph.

(2) Criminal and related grounds.—

(A) Conviction of certain crimes.—

(i) In general.— Except as provided in clause (ii), any alien convicted of, or who admits having committed, or who admits committing acts which constitute the essential elements of—

(I) a crime involving moral turpitude (other than a purely political offense) or an attempt or conspiracy to commit such a crime, or

(II) a violation of (or a conspiracy or attempt to violate) any law or regulation of a State, the United States, or a foreign country relating to a controlled substance (as defined in section 802 of title 21),

is inadmissible.

(ii) Exception.—Clause (i)(I) shall not apply to an alien who committed only one crime if—

(I) the crime was committed when the alien was under 18 years of age, and the crime was committed (and the alien released from any confinement to a prison or correctional institution imposed for the crime) more than 5 years before the date of application for a visa or other documentation and the date of application for admission to the United States, or

(II) the maximum penalty possible for the crime of which the alien was convicted (or which the alien admits having committed or of which the acts that the alien admits having committed constituted the essential elements) did not exceed imprisonment for one year and, if the alien was convicted of such crime, the alien was not sentenced to a term of imprisonment in excess of 6 months (regardless of the extent to which the sentence was ultimately executed).

(B) Multiple criminal convictions.—

Any alien convicted of 2 or more offenses (other than purely political offenses), regardless of whether the conviction was in a single trial or whether the offenses arose from a single scheme of misconduct and regardless of whether the offenses involved moral turpitude, for which the aggregate sentences to confinement were 5 years or more is inadmissible.

(C) Controlled substance traffickers.—

Any alien who the consular officer or the Attorney General knows or has reason to believe—

(i) is or has been an illicit trafficker in any controlled substance or in any listed chemical (as defined in section 802 of title 21), or is or has been a knowing aider, abettor, assister, conspirator, or colluder with others in the illicit trafficking in any such controlled or listed substance or chemical, or endeavored to do so; or

(ii) is the spouse, son, or daughter of an alien inadmissible under clause (i), has, within the previous 5 years, obtained any financial or other benefit from the illicit activity of that alien, and knew or reasonably should have known that the financial or other benefit was the product of such illicit activity,

is inadmissible.

(D) Prostitution and commercialized vice.—

Any alien who—

(i) is coming to the United States solely, principally, or incidentally to engage in prostitution, or has engaged in prostitution within 10 years of the date of application for a visa, admission, or adjustment of status,

(ii) directly or indirectly procures or attempts to procure, or (within 10 years of the date of application for a visa, admission, or adjustment of status) procured or attempted to procure or to import, prostitutes or persons for the purpose of prostitution, or receives or (within such 10-year period) received, in whole or in part, the proceeds of prostitution, or

(iii) is coming to the United States to engage in any other unlawful commercialized vice, whether or not related to prostitution,

is inadmissible.

(E) Certain aliens involved in serious criminal activity who have asserted immunity from prosecution.—

Any alien—

(i) who has committed in the United States at any time a serious criminal offense (as defined in section 1101 (h) of this title),

(ii) for whom immunity from criminal jurisdiction was exercised with respect to that offense,

(iii) who as a consequence of the offense and exercise of immunity has departed from the United States, and

(iv) who has not subsequently submitted fully to the jurisdiction of the court in the United States having jurisdiction with respect to that offense,

is inadmissible.

(F) Waiver authorized.— For provision authorizing waiver of certain subparagraphs of this paragraph, see subsection (h) of this section.

(G) Foreign government officials who have committed particularly severe violations of religious freedom.—

Any alien who, while serving as a foreign government official, was responsible for or directly carried out, at any time, particularly severe violations of religious freedom, as defined in section 6402 of title 22, is inadmissible.

(H) Significant traffickers in persons.—

(i) In general.— Any alien who commits or conspires to commit human trafficking offenses in the United States or outside the United States, or who the consular officer, the Secretary of Homeland Security, the Secretary of State, or the Attorney General knows or has reason to believe is or has been a knowing aider, abettor, assister, conspirator, or colluder with such a trafficker in severe forms of trafficking in persons, as defined in the section 7102 of title 22, is inadmissible.

(ii) Beneficiaries of trafficking.— Except as provided in clause (iii), any alien who the consular officer or the Attorney General knows or has reason to believe is the spouse, son, or daughter of an alien inadmissible under clause (i), has, within the previous 5 years, obtained any financial or other benefit from the illicit activity of that alien, and knew or reasonably should have known that the financial or other benefit was the product of such illicit activity, is inadmissible.

(iii) Exception for certain sons and daughters.— Clause (ii) shall not apply to a son or daughter who was a child at the time he or she received the benefit described in such clause.

(I) Money laundering.— Any alien—

(i) who a consular officer or the Attorney General knows, or has reason to believe, has engaged, is engaging, or seeks to enter the United States to engage, in an offense which is described in section 1956 or 1957 of title 18 (relating to laundering of monetary instruments); or

(ii) who a consular officer or the Attorney General knows is, or has been, a knowing aider, abettor, assister, conspirator, or colluder with others in an offense which is described in such section;

is inadmissible.

(3) Security and related grounds.—

(A) In general.— Any alien who a consular officer or the Attorney General knows, or has reasonable ground to believe, seeks to enter the United States to engage solely, principally, or incidentally in—

(i) any activity

(I) to violate any law of the United States relating to espionage or sabotage or

(II) to violate or evade any law prohibiting the export from the United States of goods, technology, or sensitive information,

(ii) any other unlawful activity, or

(iii) any activity a purpose of which is the opposition to, or the control or overthrow of, the Government of the United States by force, violence, or other unlawful means, is inadmissible.

(B) Terrorist activities.—

(i) In general.— Any alien who—

(I) has engaged in a terrorist activity;

(II) a consular officer, the Attorney General, or the Secretary of Homeland Security knows, or has reasonable ground to believe, is engaged in or is likely to engage after entry in any terrorist activity (as defined in clause (iv));

(III) has, under circumstances indicating an intention to cause death or serious bodily harm, incited terrorist activity;

(IV) is a representative (as defined in clause (v)) of—

(aa) a terrorist organization (as defined in clause (vi)); or

(bb) a political, social, or other group that endorses or espouses terrorist activity;

(V) is a member of a terrorist organization described in subclause (I) or (II) of clause (vi);

(VI) is a member of a terrorist organization described in clause (vi)(III), unless the alien can demonstrate by clear and convincing evidence that the alien did not know, and should not reasonably have known, that the organization was a terrorist organization;

(VII) endorses or espouses terrorist activity or persuades others to endorse or espouse terrorist activity or support a terrorist organization;

(VIII) has received military-type training (as defined in section 2339D (c)(1) of title 18) from or on behalf of any organization that, at the time the training was received, was a terrorist organization (as defined in clause (vi)); or

(IX) is the spouse or child of an alien who is inadmissible under this subparagraph, if the activity causing the alien to be found inadmissible occurred within the last 5 years,

is inadmissible. An alien who is an officer, official, representative, or spokesman of the Palestine Liberation Organization is considered, for purposes of this Act, to be engaged in a terrorist activity.

(ii) Exception.— Subclause (IX) of clause (i) does not apply to a spouse or child—

(I) who did not know or should not reasonably have known of the activity causing the alien to be found inadmissible under this section; or

(II) whom the consular officer or Attorney General has reasonable grounds to believe has renounced the activity causing the alien to be found inadmissible under this section.

(iii) "Terrorist activity" defined.— As used in this chapter, the term "terrorist activity" means any activity which is unlawful under the laws of the place where it is committed (or which, if it had been committed in the United States, would be unlawful under the laws of the United States or any State) and which involves any of the following:

(I) The highjacking or sabotage of any conveyance (including an aircraft, vessel, or vehicle).

(II) The seizing or detaining, and threatening to kill, injure, or continue to detain, another individual in order to compel a third person (including a governmental organization) to do or abstain from doing any act as an explicit or implicit condition for the release of the individual seized or detained.

(III) A violent attack upon an internationally protected person (as defined in section 1116 (b)(4) of title 18) or upon the liberty of such a person.

(IV) An assassination.

(V) The use of any—

(a) biological agent, chemical agent, or nuclear weapon or device, or

(b) explosive, firearm, or other weapon or dangerous device (other than for mere personal monetary gain), with intent to endanger, directly or indirectly, the safety of one or more individuals or to cause substantial damage to property.

(VI) A threat, attempt, or conspiracy to do any of the foregoing.

(iv) "Engage in terrorist activity" defined.— As used in this chapter, the term "engage in terrorist activity" means, in an individual capacity or as a member of an organization—

(I) to commit or to incite to commit, under circumstances indicating an intention to cause death or serious bodily injury, a terrorist activity;

(II) to prepare or plan a terrorist activity;

(III) to gather information on potential targets for terrorist activity;

(IV) to solicit funds or other things of value for—

(aa) a terrorist activity;

(bb) a terrorist organization described in clause (vi)(I) or (vi)(II); or (cc) a terrorist organization described in clause (vi)(III), unless the solicitor candemonstrate by clear and convincing evidence that he did not know, and should not reasonably have known, that the organization was a terrorist organization;

(V) to solicit any individual—

(aa) to engage in conduct otherwise described in this subsection;

(bb) for membership in a terrorist organization described in clause (vi)(I) or (vi)(II); or

(cc) for membership in a terrorist organization described in clause (vi)(III) unless the solicitor can demonstrate by clear and convincing evidence that he did not know, and should not reasonably have known, that the organization was a terrorist organization; or

(VI) to commit an act that the actor knows, or reasonably should know, affords material support, including a safe house, transportation, communications, funds, transfer of funds or other material financial benefit, false documentation or identification, weapons (including chemical, biological, or radiological weapons), explosives, or training—

(aa) for the commission of a terrorist activity;

(bb) to any individual who the actor knows, or reasonably should know, has committed or plans to commit a terrorist activity;

(cc) to a terrorist organization described in subclause (I) or (II) of clause (vi) or to any member of such an organization; or

(dd) to a terrorist organization described in clause (vi)(III), or to any member of such an organization, unless the actor can demonstrate by clear and convincing evidence that the actor did not know, and should not reasonably have known, that the organization was a terrorist organization.

(v) "Representative" defined.— As used in this paragraph, the term "representative" includes an officer, official, or spokesman of an organization, and any person who directs, counsels, commands, or induces an organization or its members to engage in terrorist activity.

(vi) "Terrorist organization" defined.— As used in this section, the term "terrorist organization" means an organization—

(I) designated under section 1189 of this title;

(II) otherwise designated, upon publication in the Federal Register, by the Secretary of State in consultation with or upon the request of the Attorney General or the Secretary of Homeland Security, as a terrorist organization, after finding that the organization engages in the activities described in subclauses (I) through (VI) of clause (iv); or

(III) that is a group of two or more individuals, whether organized or not, which engages in, or has a subgroup which engages in, the activities described in subclauses (I) through (VI) of clause (iv).

(C) Foreign policy.—

(i) In general.— An alien whose entry or proposed activities in the United States the Secretary of State has reasonable ground to believe would have potentially serious adverse foreign policy consequences for the United States is inadmissible.

(ii) Exception for officials.— An alien who is an official of a foreign government or a purported government, or who is a candidate for election to a foreign government office during the period immediately preceding the election for that office, shall not be excludable or subject to restrictions or conditions on entry into the United States under clause (i) solely because of the alien's past, current, or expected beliefs, statements, or associations, if such beliefs, statements, or associations would be lawful within the United States.

(iii) Exception for other aliens.— An alien, not described in clause (ii), shall not be excludable or subject to restrictions or conditions on entry into the United States under clause (i) because of the alien's past, current, or expected beliefs, statements, or associations, if such beliefs, statements, or associations would be lawful within the United States, unless the Secretary of State personally determines that the alien's admission would compromise a compelling United States foreign policy interest.

(iv) Notification of determinations.— If a determination is made under clause (iii) with respect to an alien, the Secretary of State must notify on a timely basis the chairmen of the Committees on the Judiciary and Foreign Affairs of the House of Representatives and of the Committees on the Judiciary and Foreign Relations of the Senate of the identity of the alien and the reasons for the determination.

(D) Immigrant membership in totalitarian party.—

(i) In general.— Any immigrant who is or has been a member of or affiliated with the Communist or any other totalitarian party (or subdivision or affiliate thereof), domestic or foreign, is inadmissible.

(ii) Exception for involuntary membership.— Clause (i) shall not apply to an alien because of membership or affiliation if the alien establishes to the satisfaction of the consular officer when applying for a visa (or to the satisfaction of the Attorney General when applying for admission) that the membership or affiliation is or was involuntary, or is or was solely when under 16 years of age, by operation of law, or for purposes of obtaining employment, food rations, or other essentials of living and whether necessary for such purposes.

(iii) Exception for past membership.— Clause (i) shall not apply to an alien because of membership or affiliation if the alien establishes to the satisfaction of the consular officer when applying for a visa (or to the satisfaction of the Attorney General when applying for admission) that—

(I) the membership or affiliation terminated at least—

(a) 2 years before the date of such application, or

(b) 5 years before the date of such application, in the case of an alien whose membership or affiliation was with the party controlling the government of a foreign state that is a totalitarian dictatorship as of such date, and

(II) the alien is not a threat to the security of the United States.

(iv) Exception for close family members.— The Attorney General may, in the Attorney General's discretion, waive the application of clause (i) in the case of an immigrant who is the parent, spouse, son, daughter, brother, or sister of a citizen of the United States or a spouse, son, or daughter of an alien lawfully admitted for permanent residence for humanitarian purposes, to assure family unity, or when it is otherwise in the public interest if the immigrant is not a threat to the security of the United States.

(E) Participants in Nazi persecution, genocide, or the commission of any act of torture or extrajudicial killing.—

(i) Participation in Nazi persecutions.— Any alien who, during the period beginning on March 23, 1933, and ending on May 8, 1945, under the direction of, or in association with—

(I) the Nazi government of Germany,

(II) any government in any area occupied by the military forces of the Nazi government of Germany,

(III) any government established with the assistance or cooperation of the Nazi government of Germany, or

(IV) any government which was an ally of the Nazi government of Germany,

ordered, incited, assisted, or otherwise participated in the persecution of any person because of race, religion, national origin, or political opinion is inadmissible.

(ii) Participation in genocide.— Any alien who ordered, incited, assisted, or otherwise participated in conduct outside the United States that would, if committed in the United States or by a United States national, be genocide, as defined in section 1091 (a) of title 18, is inadmissible.

(iii) Commission of acts of torture or extrajudicial killings.— Any alien who, outside the United States, has committed, ordered, incited, assisted, or otherwise participated in the commission of—

(I) any act of torture, as defined in section 2340 of title 18; or

(II) under color of law of any foreign nation, any extrajudicial killing, as defined in section 3(a) of the Torture Victim Protection Act of 1991 (28 U.S.C. 1350 note),

is inadmissible.

(F) Association with terrorist organizations.— Any alien who the Secretary of State, after consultation with the Attorney General, or the Attorney General, after consultation with the Secretary of State, determines has been associated with a terrorist organization and intends while in the United States to engage solely, principally, or incidentally in activities that could endanger the welfare, safety, or security of the United States is inadmissible.

(G) Recruitment or use of child soldiers.— Any alien who has engaged in the recruitment or use of child soldiers in violation of section 2442 of title 18 is inadmissible.

(4) Public charge.—

(A) In general.— Any alien who, in the opinion of the consular officer at the time of application for a visa, or in the opinion of the Attorney General at the time of application for admission or adjustment of status, is likely at any time to become a public charge is inadmissible.

(B) Factors to be taken into account.—

(i) In determining whether an alien is inadmissible under this paragraph, the consular officer or the Attorney General shall at a minimum consider the alien's—

(I) age;

(II) health;

(III) family status;

(IV) assets, resources, and financial status; and

(V) education and skills.

(ii) In addition to the factors under clause (i), the consular officer or the Attorney General may also consider any affidavit of support under section 1183a of this title for purposes of exclusion under this paragraph.

(C) Family-sponsored immigrants.— Any alien who seeks admission or adjustment of status under a visa number issued under section 1151 (b)(2) or 1153 (a) of this title is inadmissible under this paragraph unless—

(i) the alien has obtained–

(I) status as a spouse or a child of a United States citizen pursuant to clause (ii), (iii), or (iv) of section 1154 (a)(1)(A) of this title;

(II) classification pursuant to clause (ii) or (iii) of section 1154 (a)(1)(B) of this title; or

(III) classification or status as a VAWA self-petitioner; or

(ii) the person petitioning for the alien's admission (and any additional sponsor required under section 1183a (f) of this title or any alternative sponsor permitted under paragraph (5)(B) of such section) has executed an affidavit of support described in section 1183a of this title with respect to such alien.

(D) Certain employment-based immigrants.– Any alien who seeks admission or adjustment of status under a visa number issued under section 1153 (b) of this title by virtue of a classification petition filed by a relative of the alien (or by an entity in which such relative has a significant ownership interest) is inadmissible under this paragraph unless such relative has executed an affidavit of support described in section 1183a of this title with respect to such alien.

(5) Labor certification and qualifications for certain immigrants.–

(A) Labor certification.–

(i) In general-- Any alien who seeks to enter the United States for the purpose of performing skilled or unskilled labor is inadmissible, unless the Secretary of Labor has determined and certified to the Secretary of State and the Attorney General that–

(I) there are not sufficient workers who are able, willing, qualified (or equally qualified in the case of an alien described in clause (ii)) and available at the time of application for a visa and admission to the United States and at the place where the alien is to perform such skilled or unskilled labor, and

(II) the employment of such alien will not adversely affect the wages and working conditions of workers in the United States similarly employed.

(ii) Certain aliens subject to special rule.– For purposes of clause (i)(I), an alien described in this clause is an alien who–

(I) is a member of the teaching profession, or

(II) has exceptional ability in the sciences or the arts.

(iii) Professional athletes.–

(I) In general.– A certification made under clause (i) with respect to a professional athlete shall remain valid with respect to the athlete after the athlete changes employer, if the new employer is a team in the same sport as the team which employed the athlete when the athlete first applied for the certification.

(II) "Professional athlete" defined.– For purposes of subclause (I), the term "professional athlete" means an individual who is employed as an athlete by–

(aa) a team that is a member of an association of 6 or more professional sports teams whose total combined revenues exceed $10,000,000 per year, if the association governs the conduct of its members and regulates the contests and exhibitions in which its member teams regularly engage; or

(bb) any minor league team that is affiliated with such an association.

(iv) Long delayed adjustment applicants.– A certification made under clause (i) with respect to an individual whose petition is covered by section 1154 (j) of this title shall remain valid with respect to a new job accepted by the individual after the individual changes jobs or employers if the new job is in the same or a similar occupational classification as the job for which the certification was issued.

(B) Unqualified physicians.– An alien who is a graduate of a medical school not accredited by a body or bodies approved for the purpose by the Secretary of Education (regardless of whether such school of medicine is in the United States) and who is coming to the United States principally to perform services as a member of the medical profession is inadmissible, unless the alien

(i) has passed parts I and II of the National Board of Medical Examiners Examination (or an equivalent examination as determined by the Secretary of Health and Human Services) and

(ii) is competent in oral and written English. For purposes of the previous sentence, an alien who is a graduate of a medical school shall be considered to have passed parts I and II of the National Board of Medical Examiners if the alien was fully and permanently licensed to practice medicine in a State on January 9, 1978, and was practicing medicine in a State on that date.

(C) Uncertified foreign health-care workers.– Subject to subsection (r) of this section, any alien who seeks to enter the United States for the purpose of performing labor as a health-care worker, other than a physician, is inadmissible unless the alien presents to the consular officer, or, in the case of an adjustment of status, the Attorney General, a certificate from the Commission on Graduates of Foreign Nursing Schools, or a certificate from an equivalent independent credentialing organization approved by the Attorney General in consultation with the Secretary of Health and Human Services, verifying that–

(i) the alien's education, training, license, and experience–

(I) meet all applicable statutory and regulatory requirements for entry into the United States under the classification specified in the application;

(II) are comparable with that required for an American health-care worker of the same type; and

(III) are authentic and, in the case of a license, unencumbered;

(ii) the alien has the level of competence in oral and written English considered by the Secretary of Health and Human Services, in consultation with the Secretary of Education, to be appropriate for health care work of the kind in which the alien will be engaged, as shown by an appropriate score on one or more nationally recognized, commercially available, standardized assessments of the applicant's ability to speak and write; and

(iii) if a majority of States licensing the profession in which the alien intends to work recognize a test predicting the success on the profession's licensing or certification examination, the alien has passed such a test or has passed such an examination.

For purposes of clause (ii), determination of the standardized tests required and of the minimum scores that are appropriate are within the sole discretion of the Secretary of Health and Human Services and are not subject to further administrative or judicial review.

(D) Application of grounds.— The grounds for inadmissibility of aliens under subparagraphs (A) and (B) shall apply to immigrants seeking admission or adjustment of status under paragraph (2) or (3) of section 1153 (b) of this title.

(6) Illegal entrants and immigration violators.—

(A) Aliens present without admission or parole.—

(i) In general.— An alien present in the United States without being admitted or paroled, or who arrives in the United States at any time or place other than as designated by the Attorney General, is inadmissible.

(ii) Exception for certain battered women and children.— Clause (i) shall not apply to an alien who demonstrates that—

(I) the alien is a VAWA self-petitioner;

(II)   (a) the alien has been battered or subjected to extreme cruelty by a spouse or parent, or by a member of the spouse's or parent's family residing in the same household as the alien and the spouse or parent consented or acquiesced to such battery or cruelty, or

(b) the alien's child has been battered or subjected to extreme cruelty by a spouse or parent of the alien (without the active participation of the alien in the battery or cruelty) or by a member of the spouse's or parent's family residing in the same household as the alien when the spouse or parent consented to or acquiesced in such battery or cruelty and the alien did not actively participate in such battery or cruelty, and

(III) there was a substantial connection between the battery or cruelty described in subclause (I) or (II) and the alien's unlawful entry into the United States.

(B) Failure to attend removal proceeding.— Any alien who without reasonable cause fails or refuses to attend or remain in attendance at a proceeding to determine the alien's inadmissibility or deportability and who seeks admission to the United States within 5 years of such alien's subsequent departure or removal is inadmissible.

(C) Misrepresentation.—

(i) In general.— Any alien who, by fraud or willfully misrepresenting a material fact, seeks to procure (or has sought to procure or has procured) a visa, other documentation, or admission into the United States or other benefit provided under this chapter is inadmissible.

(ii) Falsely claiming citizenship.—

(I) In general.— Any alien who falsely represents, or has falsely represented, himself or herself to be a citizen of the United States for any purpose or benefit under this chapter (including section 1324a of this title) or any other Federal or State law is inadmissible.

(II) Exception.— In the case of an alien making a representation described in subclause (I), if each natural parent of the alien (or, in the case of an adopted alien, each adoptive parent of the alien) is or was a citizen (whether by birth or naturalization), the alien permanently resided in the United States prior to attaining the age of 16, and the alien reasonably believed at the time of making such representation that he or she was a citizen, the alien shall not be considered to be inadmissible under any provision of this subsection based on such representation.

(iii) Waiver authorized.— For provision authorizing waiver of clause (i), see subsection (i) of this section.

(D) Stowaways.— Any alien who is a stowaway is inadmissible.

(E) Smugglers.—

(i) In general.— Any alien who at any time knowingly has encouraged, induced, assisted, abetted, or aided any other alien to enter or to try to enter the United States in violation of law is inadmissible.

(ii) Special rule in the case of family reunification.— Clause (i) shall not apply in the case of alien who is an eligible immigrant (as defined in section 301(b)(1) of the Immigration Act of 1990), was physically present in the United States on May 5, 1988, and is seeking admission as an immediate relative or under section 1153 (a)(2) of this title (including under section 112 of the Immigration Act of 1990) or benefits under section 301(a) of the Immigration Act of 1990 if the alien, before May 5, 1988, has encouraged, induced, assisted, abetted, or aided only the alien's spouse, parent, son, or daughter (and no other individual) to enter the United States in violation of law.

(iii) Waiver authorized.– For provision authorizing waiver of clause (i), see subsection (d)(11) of this section.

(F) Subject of civil penalty.–

(i) In general.– An alien who is the subject of a final order for violation of section 1324c of this title is inadmissible.

(ii) Waiver authorized.– For provision authorizing waiver of clause (i), see subsection (d)(12) of this section.

(G) Student visa abusers.– An alien who obtains the status of a nonimmigrant under section 1101 (a)(15)(F)(i) of this title and who violates a term or condition of such status under section 1184 (I) [2] of this title is inadmissible until the alien has been outside the United States for a continuous period of 5 years after the date of the violation.

(7) Documentation requirements.–

(A) Immigrants.–

(i) In general.– Except as otherwise specifically provided in this chapter, any immigrant at the time of application for admission–

(I) who is not in possession of a valid unexpired immigrant visa, reentry permit, border crossing identification card, or other valid entry document required by this chapter, and a valid unexpired passport, or other suitable travel document, or document of identity and nationality if such document is required under the regulations issued by the Attorney General under section 1181 (a) of this title, or

(II) whose visa has been issued without compliance with the provisions of section 1153 of this title, is inadmissible.

(ii) Waiver authorized.– For provision authorizing waiver of clause (i), see subsection (k) of this section.

(B) Nonimmigrants.–

(i) In general.– Any nonimmigrant who–

(I) is not in possession of a passport valid for a minimum of six months from the date of the expiration of the initial period of the alien's admission or contemplated initial period of stay authorizing the alien to return to the country from which the alien came or to proceed to and enter some other country during such period, or

(II) is not in possession of a valid nonimmigrant visa or border crossing identification card at the time of application for admission, is inadmissible.

(ii) General waiver authorized.– For provision authorizing waiver of clause (i), see subsection (d)(4) of this section.

(iii) Guam and Northern Mariana Islands visa waiver.– For provision authorizing waiver of clause (i) in the case of visitors to Guam or the Commonwealth of the Northern Mariana Islands, see subsection (I).

(iv) Visa waiver program.– For authority to waive the requirement of clause (i) under a program, see section 1187 of this title.

(8) Ineligible for citizenship.–

(A) In general.– Any immigrant who is permanently ineligible to citizenship is inadmissible.

(B) Draft evaders.– Any person who has departed from or who has remained outside the United States to avoid or evade training or service in the armed forces in time of war or a period declared by the President to be a national emergency is inadmissible, except that this subparagraph shall not apply to an alien who at the time of such departure was a nonimmigrant and who is seeking to reenter the United States as a nonimmigrant.

(9) Aliens previously removed.–

(A) Certain aliens previously removed.–

(i) Arriving aliens.– Any alien who has been ordered removed under section 1225 (b)(1) of this title or at the end of proceedings under section 1229a of this title initiated upon the alien's arrival in the United States and who again seeks admission within 5 years of the date of such removal (or within 20 years in the case of a second or subsequent removal or at any time in the case of an alien convicted of an aggravated felony) is inadmissible.

(ii) Other aliens.– Any alien not described in clause (i) who–

(I) has been ordered removed under section 1229a of this title or any other provision of law, or

(II) departed the United States while an order of removal was outstanding,

and who seeks admission within 10 years of the date of such alien's departure or removal (or within 20 years of such date in the case of a second or subsequent removal or at any time in the case of an alien convicted of an aggravated felony) is inadmissible.

(iii) Exception.— Clauses (i) and (ii) shall not apply to an alien seeking admission within a period if, prior to the date of the alien's reembarkation at a place outside the United States or attempt to be admitted from foreign contiguous territory, the Attorney General has consented to the alien's re-applying for admission.

(B) Aliens unlawfully present.—

(i) In general.— Any alien (other than an alien lawfully admitted for permanent residence) who—

(I) was unlawfully present in the United States for a period of more than 180 days but less than 1 year, voluntarily departed the United States (whether or not pursuant to section 1254a (e) [3] of this title) prior to the commencement of proceedings under section 1225 (b)(1) of this title or section 1229a of this title, and again seeks admission within 3 years of the date of such alien's departure or removal, or

(II) has been unlawfully present in the United States for one year or more, and who again seeks admission within 10 years of the date of such alien's departure or removal from the United States,

is inadmissible.

(ii) Construction of unlawful presence.— For purposes of this paragraph, an alien is deemed to be unlawfully present in the United States if the alien is present in the United States after the expiration of the period of stay authorized by the Attorney General or is present in the United States without being admitted or paroled.

(iii) Exceptions.—

(I) Minors.— No period of time in which an alien is under 18 years of age shall be taken into account in determining the period of unlawful presence in the United States under clause (i).

(II) Asylees.—No period of time in which an alien has a bona fide application for asylum pending under section 1158 of this title shall be taken into account in determining the period of unlawful presence in the United States under clause (i) unless the alien during such period was employed without authorization in the United States.

(III) Family unity.—No period of time in which the alien is a beneficiary of family unity protection pursuant to section 301 of the Immigration Act of 1990 shall be taken into account in determining the period of unlawful presence in the United States under clause (i).

(IV) Battered women and children.— Clause (i) shall not apply to an alien who would be described in paragraph (6)(A)(ii) if "violation of the terms of the alien's nonimmigrant visa" were substituted for "unlawful entry into the United States" in subclause (III) of that paragraph.

(V) Victims of a severe form of trafficking in persons.— Clause (i) shall not apply to an alien who demonstrates that the severe form of trafficking (as that term is defined in section 7102 of title 22) was at least one central reason for the alien's unlawful presence in the United States.

(iv) Tolling for good cause.— In the case of an alien who—

(I) has been lawfully admitted or paroled into the United States,

(II) has filed a nonfrivolous application for a change or extension of status before the date of expiration of the period of stay authorized by the Attorney General, and

(III) has not been employed without authorization in the United States before or during the pendency of such application,

the calculation of the period of time specified in clause (i)(I) shall be tolled during the pendency of such application, but not to exceed 120 days.

(v) Waiver.— The Attorney General has sole discretion to waive clause (i) in the case of an immigrant who is the spouse or son or daughter of a United States citizen or of an alien lawfully admitted for permanent residence, if it is established to the satisfaction of the Attorney General that the refusal of admission to such immigrant alien would result in extreme hardship to the citizen or lawfully resident spouse or parent of such alien. No court shall have jurisdiction to review a decision or action by the Attorney General regarding a waiver under this clause.

(C) Aliens unlawfully present after previous immigration violations.—

(i) In general.— Any alien who—

(I) has been unlawfully present in the United States for an aggregate period of more than 1 year, or

(II) has been ordered removed under section 1225 (b)(1) of this title, section 1229a of this title, or any other provision of law,

and who enters or attempts to reenter the United States without being admitted is inadmissible.

(ii) Exception.— Clause (i) shall not apply to an alien seeking admission more than 10 years after the date of the alien's last departure from the United States if, prior to the alien's reembarkation at a place outside the United States or attempt to be readmitted from a foreign contiguous territory, the Secretary of Homeland Security has consented to the alien's reapplying for admission.

(iii) Waiver.— The Secretary of Homeland Security may waive the application of clause (i) in the case of an alien who is a VAWA self-petitioner if there is a connection between—

(I) the alien's battering or subjection to extreme cruelty; and

(II) the alien's removal, departure from the United States, reentry or reentries into the United States; or attempted reentry into the United States.

(10) Miscellaneous.—

(A) Practicing polygamists.— Any immigrant who is coming to the United States to practice polygamy is inadmissible.

(B) Guardian required to accompany helpless alien.— Any alien—

(i) who is accompanying another alien who is inadmissible and who is certified to be helpless from sickness, mental or physical disability, or infancy pursuant to section 1222 (c) of this title, and

(ii) whose protection or guardianship is determined to be required by the alien described in clause (i),

is inadmissible.

(C) International child abduction.—

(i) In general.— Except as provided in clause (ii), any alien who, after entry of an order by a court in the United States granting custody to a person of a United States citizen child who detains or retains the child, or withholds custody of the child, outside the United States from the person granted custody by that order, is inadmissible until the child is surrendered to the person granted custody by that order.

(ii) Aliens supporting abductors and relatives of abductors.— Any alien who—

(I) is known by the Secretary of State to have intentionally assisted an alien in the conduct described in clause (i),

(II) is known by the Secretary of State to be intentionally providing material support or safe haven to an alien described in clause (i), or

(III) is a spouse (other than the spouse who is the parent of the abducted child), child (other than the abducted child), parent, sibling, or agent of an alien described in clause (i), if such person has been designated by the Secretary of State at the Secretary's sole and unreviewable discretion, is inadmissible until the child described in clause (i) is surrendered to the person granted custody by the order described in that clause, and such person and child are permitted to return to the United States or such person's place of residence.

(iii) Exceptions.— Clauses (i) and (ii) shall not apply—

(I) to a government official of the United States who is acting within the scope of his or her official duties;

(II) to a government official of any foreign government if the official has been designated by the Secretary of State at the Secretary's sole and unreviewable discretion; or

(III) so long as the child is located in a foreign state that is a party to the Convention on the Civil Aspects of International Child Abduction, done at The Hague on October 25, 1980.

(D) Unlawful voters.—

(i) In general.— Any alien who has voted in violation of any Federal, State, or local constitutional provision, statute, ordinance, or regulation is inadmissible.

(ii) Exception.— In the case of an alien who voted in a Federal, State, or local election (including an initiative, recall, or referendum) in violation of a lawful restriction of voting to citizens, if each natural parent of the alien (or, in the case of an adopted alien, each adoptive parent of the alien) is or was a citizen (whether by birth or naturalization), the alien permanently resided in the United States prior to attaining the age of 16, and the alien reasonably believed at the time of such violation that he or she was a citizen, the alien shall not be considered to be inadmissible under any provision of this subsection based on such violation.

(E) Former citizens who renounced citizenship to avoid taxation.— Any alien who is a former citizen of the United States who officially renounces United States citizenship and who is determined by the Attorney General to have renounced United States citizenship for the purpose of avoiding taxation by the United States is inadmissible.

General Grounds of Deportability under the Immigration & Nationality Act
INA Section 237 (8 U.S.C. § 1227)

(a) Classes of deportable aliens.— Any alien (including an alien crewman) in and admitted to the United States shall, upon the order of the Attorney General, be removed if the alien is within one or more of the following classes of deportable aliens:

(1) Inadmissible at time of entry or of adjustment of status or violates status.—

(A) Inadmissible aliens.— Any alien who at the time of entry or adjustment of status was within one or more of the classes of aliens inadmissible by the law existing at such time is deportable.

(B) Present in violation of law.– Any alien who is present in the United States in violation of this chapter or any other law of the United States, or whose nonimmigrant visa (or other documentation authorizing admission into the United States as a nonimmigrant) has been revoked under section 1201 (i) of this title, is deportable.

(C) Violated nonimmigrant status or condition of entry.–

(i) Nonimmigrant status violators.– Any alien who was admitted as a nonimmigrant and who has failed to maintain the nonimmigrant status in which the alien was admitted or to which it was changed under section 1258 of this title, or to comply with the conditions of any such status, is deportable.

(ii) Violators of conditions of entry.– Any alien whom the Secretary of Health and Human Services certifies has failed to comply with terms, conditions, and controls that were imposed under section 1182 (g) of this title is deportable.

(D) Termination of conditional permanent residence.–

(i) In general.– Any alien with permanent resident status on a conditional basis under section 1186a of this title (relating to conditional permanent resident status for certain alien spouses and sons and daughters) or under section 1186b of this title (relating to conditional permanent resident status for certain alien entrepreneurs, spouses, and children) who has had such status terminated under such respective section is deportable.

(ii) Exception.– Clause (i) shall not apply in the cases described in section 1186a (c)(4) of this title (relating to certain hardship waivers).

(E) Smuggling.–

(i) In general.– Any alien who (prior to the date of entry, at the time of any entry, or within 5 years of the date of any entry) knowingly has encouraged, induced, assisted, abetted, or aided any other alien to enter or to try to enter the United States in violation of law is deportable.

(ii) Special rule in the case of family reunification.– Clause (i) shall not apply in the case of alien who is an eligible immigrant (as defined in section 301(b)(1) of the Immigration Act of 1990), was physically present in the United States on May 5, 1988, and is seeking admission as an immediate relative or under section 1153 (a)(2) of this title (including under section 112 of the Immigration Act of 1990) or benefits under section 301(a) of the Immigration Act of 1990 if the alien, before May 5, 1988, has encouraged, induced, assisted, abetted, or aided only the alien's spouse, parent, son, or daughter (and no other individual) to enter the United States in violation of law.

(iii) Waiver authorized.– The Attorney General may, in his discretion for humanitarian purposes, to assure family unity, or when it is otherwise in the public interest, waive application of clause (i) in the case of any alien lawfully admitted for permanent residence if the alien has encouraged, induced, assisted, abetted, or aided only an individual who at the time of the offense was the alien's spouse, parent, son, or daughter (and no other individual) to enter the United States in violation of law.

(F) [Repealed. Pub. L. 104–208, div. C, title VI, § 671(d)(1)(C), Sept. 30, 1996, 110 Stat. 3009–723]

(G) Marriage fraud.–An alien shall be considered to be deportable as having procured a visa or other documentation by fraud (within the meaning of section 1182 (a)(6)(C)(i) of this title) and to be in the United States in violation of this chapter (within the meaning of subparagraph (B)) if–

(i) the alien obtains any admission into the United States with an immigrant visa or other documentation procured on the basis of a marriage entered into less than 2 years prior to such admission of the alien and which, within 2 years subsequent to any admission of the alien in the United States, shall be judicially annulled or terminated, unless the alien establishes to the satisfaction of the Attorney General that such marriage was not contracted for the purpose of evading any provisions of the immigration laws, or

(ii) it appears to the satisfaction of the Attorney General that the alien has failed or refused to fulfill the alien's marital agreement which in the opinion of the AttorneyGeneral was made for the purpose of procuring the alien's admission as an immigrant.

(H) Waiver authorized for certain misrepresentations.– The provisions of this paragraph relating to the removal of aliens within the United States on the ground that they were inadmissible at the time of admission as aliens described in section 1182 (a)(6)(C)(i) of this title, whether willful or innocent, may, in the discretion of the Attorney General, be waived for any alien (other than an alien described in paragraph (4)(D)) who–

(i)   (I) is the spouse, parent, son, or daughter of a citizen of the United States or of an alien lawfully admitted to the United States for permanent residence; and

(II) was in possession of an immigrant visa or equivalent document and was otherwise admissible to the United States at the time of such admission except for those grounds of inadmissibility specified under paragraphs (5)(A) and (7)(A) of section 1182 (a) of this title which were a direct result of that fraud or misrepresentation.

(ii) is a VAWA self-petitioner.

A waiver of removal for fraud or misrepresentation granted under this subparagraph shall also operate to waive removal based on the grounds of inadmissibility directly resulting from such fraud or misrepresentation.

(2) Criminal offenses.–

(A) General crimes.–

(i) Crimes of moral turpitude.– Any alien who–

(I) is convicted of a crime involving moral turpitude committed within five years (or 10 years in the case of an alien provided lawful permanent resident status under section 1255 (j) of this title) after the date of admission, and

(II) is convicted of a crime for which a sentence of one year or longer may be imposed,

is deportable.

(ii) Multiple criminal convictions.– Any alien who at any time after admission is convicted of two or more crimes involving moral turpitude, not arising out of a single scheme of criminal misconduct, regardless of whether confined therefor and regardless of whether the convictions were in a single trial, is deportable.

(iii) Aggravated felony.– Any alien who is convicted of an aggravated felony at any time after admission is deportable.

(iv) High speed flight.– Any alien who is convicted of a violation of section 758 of title 18 (relating to high speed flight from an immigration checkpoint) is deportable.

(v) Failure to register as a sex offender.– Any alien who is convicted under section 2250 of title 18 is deportable.

(vi) Waiver authorized.– Clauses (i), (ii), (iii), and (iv) shall not apply in the case of an alien with respect to a criminal conviction if the alien subsequent to the criminal conviction has been granted a full and unconditional pardon by the President of the United States or by the Governor of any of the several States.

(B) Controlled substances.–

(i) Conviction.– Any alien who at any time after admission has been convicted of a violation of (or a conspiracy or attempt to violate) any law or regulation of a State, the United States, or a foreign country relating to a controlled substance (as defined in section 802 of title 21), other than a single offense involving possession for one's own use of 30 grams or less of marijuana, is deportable.

(ii) Drug abusers and addicts.– Any alien who is, or at any time after admission has been, a drug abuser or addict is deportable.

(C) Certain firearm offenses.– Any alien who at any time after admission is convicted under any law of purchasing, selling, offering for sale, exchanging, using, owning, possessing, or carrying, or of attempting or conspiring to purchase, sell, offer for sale, exchange, use, own, possess, or carry, any weapon, part, or accessory which is a firearm or destructive device (as defined in section 921 (a) of title 18) in violation of any law is deportable.

(D) Miscellaneous crimes.– Any alien who at any time has been convicted (the judgment on such conviction becoming final) of, or has been so convicted of a conspiracy or attempt to violate–

(i) any offense under chapter 37 (relating to espionage), chapter 105 (relating to sabotage), or chapter 115 (relating to treason and sedition) of title 18 for which a term of imprisonment of five or more years may be imposed;

(ii) any offense under section 871 or 960 of title 18;

(iii) a violation of any provision of the Military Selective Service Act (50 App. U.S.C. 451 et seq.) or the Trading With the Enemy Act (50 App. U.S.C. 1 et seq.); or

(iv) a violation of section 1185 or 1328 of this title,

is deportable.

(E) Crimes of domestic violence, stalking, or violation of protection order, crimes against children and.–

(i) Domestic violence, stalking, and child abuse.– Any alien who at any time after admission is convicted of a crime of domestic violence, a crime of stalking, or a crime of child abuse, child neglect, or child abandonment is deportable. For purposes of this clause, the term "crime of domestic violence" means any crime of violence (as defined in section 16 of title 18) against a person committed by a current or former spouse of the person, by an individual with whom the person shares a child in common, by an individual who is cohabiting with or has cohabited with the person as a spouse, by an individual similarly situated to a spouse of the person under the domestic or family violence laws of the jurisdiction where the offense occurs, or by any other individual against a person who is protected from that individual's acts under the domestic or family violence laws of the United States or any State, Indian tribal government, or unit of local government.

(ii) Violators of protection orders.– Any alien who at any time after admission is enjoined under a protection order issued by a court and whom the court determines has engaged in conduct that violates the portion of a protection order that involves protection against credible threats of violence, repeated harassment, or bodily injury to the person or persons for whom the protection order was issued is deportable. For purposes of this clause, the term "protection order" means any injunction issued for the purpose of preventing violent or threatening acts of domestic violence, including temporary or final orders issued by civil or criminal courts (other than support or child custody orders or provisions) whether obtained by filing an independent action or as a pendente lite order in another proceeding.

(F) Trafficking.– Any alien described in section 1182 (a)(2)(H) of this title is deportable.

(3) Failure to register and falsification of documents.–

(A) Change of address.— An alien who has failed to comply with the provisions of section 1305 of this title is deportable, unless the alien establishes to the satisfaction of the Attorney General that such failure was reasonably excusable or was not willful.

(B) Failure to register or falsification of documents.— Any alien who at any time has been convicted—

(i) under section 1306 (c) of this title or under section 36(c) of the Alien Registration Act, 1940,

(ii) of a violation of, or an attempt or a conspiracy to violate, any provision of the Foreign Agents Registration Act of 1938 (22 U.S.C. 611 et seq.), or

(iii) of a violation of, or an attempt or a conspiracy to violate, section 1546 of title 18 (relating to fraud and misuse of visas, permits, and other entry documents),

is deportable.

(C) Document fraud.—

(i) In general.— An alien who is the subject of a final order for violation of section 1324c of this title is deportable.

(ii) Waiver authorized.— The Attorney General may waive clause (i) in the case of an alien lawfully admitted for permanent residence if no previous civil money penalty was imposed against the alien under section 1324c of this title and the offense was incurred solely to assist, aid, or support the alien's spouse or child (and no other individual). No court shall have jurisdiction to review a decision of the Attorney General to grant or deny a waiver under this clause.

(D) Falsely claiming citizenship.—

(i) In general.— Any alien who falsely represents, or has falsely represented, himself to be a citizen of the United States for any purpose or benefit under this chapter (including section 1324a of this title) or any Federal or State law is deportable.

(ii) Exception.— In the case of an alien making a representation described in clause (i), if each natural parent of the alien (or, in the case of an adopted alien, each adoptive parent of the alien) is or was a citizen (whether by birth or naturalization), the alien permanently resided in the United States prior to attaining the age of 16, and the alien reasonably believed at the time of making such representation that he or she was a citizen, the alien shall not be considered to be deportable under any provision of this subsection based on such representation.

(4) Security and related grounds.—

(A) In general.— Any alien who has engaged, is engaged, or at any time after admission engages in—

(i) any activity to violate any law of the United States relating to espionage or sabotage or to violate or evade any law prohibiting the export from the United States of goods, technology, or sensitive information,

(ii) any other criminal activity which endangers public safety or national security, or

(iii) any activity a purpose of which is the opposition to, or the control or overthrow of, the Government of the United States by force, violence, or other unlawful means,

is deportable.

(B) Terrorist activities.— Any alien who is described in subparagraph (B) or (F) of section 1182 (a)(3) of this title is deportable.

(C) Foreign policy.—

(i) In general.— An alien whose presence or activities in the United States the Secretary of State has reasonable ground to believe would have potentially serious adverse foreign policy consequences for the United States is deportable.

(ii) Exceptions.— The exceptions described in clauses (ii) and (iii) of section 1182 (a)(3)(C) of this title shall apply to deportability under clause (i) in the same manner as they apply to inadmissibility under section 1182 (a)(3)(C)(i) of this title.

(D) Participated in Nazi persecution, genocide, or the commission of any act of torture or extrajudicial killing.— Any alien described in clause (i), (ii), or (iii) of section 1182 (a)(3)(E) of this title is deportable.

(E) Participated in the commission of severe violations of religious freedom.— Any alien described in section 1182 (a)(2)(G) of this title is deportable.

(F) Recruitment or use of child soldiers.— Any alien who has engaged in the recruitment or use of child soldiers in violation of section 2442 of title 18 is deportable.

(5) Public charge.— Any alien who, within five years after the date of entry, has become a public charge from causes not affirmatively shown to have arisen since entry is deportable.

(6) Unlawful voters.—

(A) In general.— Any alien who has voted in violation of any Federal, State, or local constitutional provision, statute, ordinance, or regulation is deportable.

(B) Exception.—

In the case of an alien who voted in a Federal, State, or local election (including an initiative, recall, or referendum) in violation of a lawful restriction of voting to citizens, if each natural parent of the alien (or, in the case of an adopted alien, each adoptive parent of the alien) is or was a citizen (whether by birth or naturalization), the alien permanently resided in the United States prior to attaining the age of 16, and the alien reasonably believed at the time of such violation that he or she was a citizen, the alien shall not be considered to be deportable under any provision of this subsection based on such violation.

(7) Waiver for victims of domestic violence.—

(A) In general.— The Attorney General is not limited by the criminal court record and may waive the application of paragraph (2)(E)(i) (with respect to crimes of domestic violence and crimes of stalking) and (ii) in the case of an alien who has been battered or subjected to extreme cruelty and who is not and was not the primary perpetrator of violence in the relationship—

    (i) upon a determination that—

        (I) the alien was acting is self-defense;

        (II) the alien was found to have violated a protection order intended to protect the alien; or

        (III) the alien committed, was arrested for, was convicted of, or pled guilty to committing a crime—

            (aa) that did not result in serious bodily injury; and

            (bb) where there was a connection between the crime and the alien's having been battered or subjected to extreme cruelty.

(B) Credible evidence considered.— In acting on applications under this paragraph, the Attorney General shall consider any credible evidence relevant to the application. The determination of what evidence is credible and the weight to be given that evidence shall be within the sole discretion of the Attorney General.

(b) Deportation of certain nonimmigrants.— An alien, admitted as a nonimmigrant under the provision of either section 1101 (a)(15)(A)(i) or 1101 (a)(15)(G)(i) of this title, and who fails to maintain a status under either of those provisions, shall not be required to depart from the United States without the approval of the Secretary of State, unless such alien is subject to deportation under paragraph (4) of subsection (a) of this section.

(c) Waiver of grounds for deportation.— Paragraphs (1)(A), (1)(B), (1)(C), (1)(D), and (3)(A) of subsection (a) of this section (other than so much of paragraph (1) as relates to a ground of inadmissibility described in paragraph (2) or (3) of section 1182 (a) of this title) shall not apply to a special immigrant described in section 1101 (a)(27)(J) of this title based upon circumstances that existed before the date the alien was provided such special immigrant status.

B. Current State Department Lists of Tier I and Tier II organizations

Current List of Designated Foreign Terrorist Organizations ("Tier I" groups)

(i)   Abu Nidal Organization (ANO)

(ii)   Abu Sayyaf Group

(iii)   Al-Aqsa Martyrs Brigade

(iv)   Al-Shabaab

(v)   Ansar al-Islam

(vi)   Armed Islamic Group (GIA)

(vii)   Asbat al-Ansar

(viii) Aum Shinrikyo

(ix)   Basque Fatherland and Liberty (ETA)

(x)   Communist Party of the Philippines/New People's Army (CPP/NPA)

(xi)   Continuity Irish Republican Army

(xii)   Gama'a al-Islamiyya (Islamic Group)

(xiii) HAMAS (Islamic Resistance Movement)

(xiv)   Harakat ul-Jihad-i-Islami/Bangladesh (HUJI-B)

(xv)   Harakat ul-Mujahidin (HUM)

(xvi)   Hizballah (Party of God)

(xvii) Islamic Jihad Group

(xviii) Islamic Movement of Uzbekistan (IMU)

(xix)   Jaish-e-Mohammed (JEM) (Army of Mohammed)

(xx)   Jemaah Islamiya organization (JI)

(xxi)   al-Jihad (Egyptian Islamic Jihad)

(xxii) Kahane Chai (Kach)

(xxiii) Kata'ib Hizballah

(xxiv) Kongra-Gel (KGK, formerly Kurdistan Workers' Party, PKK, KADEK)

(xxv)   Lashkar-e Tayyiba (LT) (Army of the Righteous)

(xxvi) Lashkar i Jhangvi

(xxvii) Liberation Tigers of Tamil Eelam (LTTE)

(xxviii) Libyan Islamic Fighting Group (LIFG)

(xxix) Moroccan Islamic Combatant Group (GICM)

(xxx)   Mujahedin-e Khalq Organization (MEK)

(xxxi) National Liberation Army (ELN)

(xxxii) Palestine Liberation Front (PLF)

(xxxiii) Palestinian Islamic Jihad (PIJ)

(xxxiv) Popular Front for the Liberation of Palestine (PFLF)

(xxxv) PFLP-General Command (PFLP-GC)

(xxxvi) Tanzim Qa'idat al-Jihad fi Bilad al-Rafidayn (QJBR) (al-Qaida in Iraq) (formerly Jama'at al-Tawhid wa'al-Jihad, JTJ, al-Zarqawi Network)

(xxxvii) al-Qa'ida

(xxxviii) al-Qaida in the Islamic Maghreb (formerly GSPC)

(xxxix) Real IRA

(xl)   Revolutionary Armed Forces of Colombia (FARC)

(xli)   Revolutionary Nuclei (formerly ELA)

(xlii) Revolutionary Organization 17 November

(xliii) Revolutionary People's Liberation Party/Front (DHKP/C)

(xliv) Shining Path (Sendero Luminoso, SL)

(xlv)   United Self-Defense Forces of Colombia (AUC)

Terrorist Exclusion List ("Tier II" groups)

- Afghan Support Committee (a.k.a. Ahya ul Turas; a.k.a. Jamiat Ayat-ur-Rhas al Islamia; a.k.a. Jamiat Ihya ul Turath al Islamia; a.k.a. Lajnat el Masa Eidatul Afghania)
- Al Taqwa Trade, Property and Industry Company Ltd. (f.k.a. Al Taqwa Trade, Property and Industry; f.k.a. Al Taqwa Trade, Property and Industry Establishment; f.k.a. Himmat Establishment; a.k.a. Waldenberg, AG)
- Al-Hamati Sweets Bakeries
- Al-Ittihad al-Islami (AIAI)
- Al-Manar
- Al-Ma'unah
- Al-Nur Honey Center
- Al-Rashid Trust
- Al-Shifa Honey Press for Industry and Commerce
- Al-Wafa al-Igatha al-Islamia (a.k.a. Wafa Humanitarian Organization; a.k.a. Al Wafa; a.k.a. Al Wafa Organization)
- Alex Boncayao Brigade (ABB)
- Anarchist Faction for Overthrow
- Army for the Liberation of Rwanda (ALIR) (a.k.a. Interahamwe, Former Armed Forces (EX-FAR))
- Asbat al-Ansar
- Babbar Khalsa International
- Bank Al Taqwa Ltd. (a.k.a. Al Taqwa Bank; a.k.a. Bank Al Taqwa)
- Black Star

- Communist Party of Nepal (Maoist) (a.k.a. CPN(M); a.k.a. the United Revolutionary People's Council, a.k.a. the People's Liberation Army of Nepal)
- Continuity Irish Republican Army (CIRA) (a.k.a. Continuity Army Council)
- Darkazanli Company
- Dhamat Houmet Daawa Salafia (a.k.a. Group Protectors of Salafist Preaching; a.k.a. Houmat Ed Daawa Es Salifiya; a.k.a. Katibat El Ahoual; a.k.a. Protectors of the Salafist Predication; a.k.a. El-Ahoual Battalion; a.k.a. Katibat El Ahouel; a.k.a. Houmate Ed-Daawa Es-Salafia; a.k.a. the Horror Squadron; a.k.a. Djamaat Houmat Eddawa Essalafia; a.k.a. Djamaatt Houmat Ed Daawa Es Salafiya; a.k.a. Salafist Call Protectors; a.k.a. Djamaat Houmat Ed Daawa Es Salafiya; a.k.a. Houmate el Da'awaa es-Salafiyya; a.k.a. Protectors of the Salafist Call; a.k.a. Houmat ed-Daaoua es-Salafia; a.k.a. Group of Supporters of the Salafiste Trend; a.k.a. Group of Supporters of the Salafist Trend)
- Eastern Turkistan Islamic Movement (a.k.a. Eastern Turkistan Islamic Party; a.k.a. ETIM; a.k.a. ETIP)
- First of October Antifascist Resistance Group (GRAPO) (a.k.a. Grupo de Resistencia Anti-Fascista Premero De Octubre)
- Harakat ul Jihad i Islami (HUJI)
- International Sikh Youth Federation
- Islamic Army of Aden
- Islamic Renewal and Reform Organization
- Jamiat al-Ta'awun al-Islamiyya
- Jamiat ul-Mujahideen (JUM)
- Japanese Red Army (JRA)
- Jaysh-e-Mohammed
- Jayshullah
- Jerusalem Warriors
- Lashkar-e-Tayyiba (LET) (a.k.a. Army of the Righteous)
- Libyan Islamic Fighting Group
- Loyalist Volunteer Force (LVF)
- Makhtab al-Khidmat
- Moroccan Islamic Combatant Group (a.k.a. GICM; a.k.a. Groupe Islamique Combattant Marocain)
- Nada Management Organization (f.k.a. Al Taqwa Management Organization SA)
- New People's Army (NPA)
- Orange Volunteers (OV)
- People Against Gangsterism and Drugs (PAGAD)

- Red Brigades-Combatant Communist Party (BR-PCC)
- Red Hand Defenders (RHD)
- Revival of Islamic Heritage Society (Pakistan and Afghanistan offices— Kuwait office not designated) (a.k.a. Jamia Ihya ul Turath; a.k.a. Jamiat Ihia Al- Turath Al-Islamiya; a.k.a. Revival of Islamic Society Heritage on the African Continent)
- Revolutionary Proletarian Nucleus
- Revolutionary United Front (RUF)
- Salafist Group for Call and Combat (GSPC)
- The Allied Democratic Forces (ADF)
- The Islamic International Brigade (a.k.a. International Battalion, a.k.a. Islamic Peacekeeping International Brigade, a.k.a. Peacekeeping Battalion, a.k.a. The International Brigade, a.k.a. The Islamic Peacekeeping Army, a.k.a. The Islamic Peacekeeping Brigade)
- The Lord's Resistance Army (LRA)
- The Pentagon Gang
- The Riyadus-Salikhin Reconnaissance and Sabotage Battalion of Chechen Martyrs (a.k.a. Riyadus-Salikhin Reconnaissance and Sabotage Battalion, a.k.a. Riyadh-as-Saliheen, a.k.a. the Sabotage and Military Surveillance Group of the Riyadh al-Salihin Martyrs, a.k.a. Riyadus-Salikhin Reconnaissance and Sabotage Battalion of Shahids (Martyrs))
- The Special Purpose Islamic Regiment (a.k.a. the Islamic Special Purpose Regiment, a.k.a. the al-Jihad-Fisi-Sabililah Special Islamic Regiment, a.k.a. Islamic Regiment of Special Meaning)
- Tunisian Combat Group (a.k.a. GCT, a.k.a. Groupe Combattant Tunisien, a.k.a. Jama'a Combattante Tunisien, a.k.a. JCT; a.k.a. Tunisian Combatant Group)
- Turkish Hizballah
- Ulster Defense Association (a.k.a. Ulster Freedom Fighters)
- Ummah Tameer E-Nau (UTN) (a.k.a. Foundation for Construction; a.k.a. Nation Building; a.k.a. Reconstruction Foundation; a.k.a. Reconstruction of the Islamic Community; a.k.a. Reconstruction of the Muslim Ummah; a.k.a. Ummah Tameer I-Nau; a.k.a. Ummah Tameer E-Nau; a.k.a. Ummah Tameer-I-Pau)
- Youssef M. Nada & Co. Gesellschaft M.B.H.

C. Sample DHS Denial of Asylee's Long-Pending Permanent Residence Application

Page 1 of 2

U.S. Department of Homeland Security
P.O. Box 82521
Lincoln, NE 68501-2521

U.S. Citizenship and Immigration Services

February 15, 2008

Refer To File No.

A

Dear Sir or Madam:

RE: Form I485 APPLICATION TO ADJUST TO PERMANENT RESIDENT STATUS
    Beneficiary:

Decision

This notice refers to the Form I-485, Application to Register Permanent Residence or Adjust Status, you filed with this office on March 22, 1999. You are requesting an adjustment of status under Section 209 of the Immigration and Nationality Act (INA) (Title 8, United States Code, section 1159).

Section 209(b) of the INA states:

The Secretary of Homeland Security or the Attorney General, in the Secretary's or the Attorney General's discretion and under such regulations as the Secretary or the Attorney General may prescribe, may adjust to the status of an alien lawfully admitted for permanent residence the status of any alien granted asylum who-

(1) applies for such adjustment,
(2) has been physically present in the United States for at least one year after being granted asylum,
(3) continues to be a refugee within the meaning of [INA] section 101(a)(42)(A) of this title or a spouse or child of such a refugee,
(4) is not firmly resettled in any foreign country, and
(5) is admissible (except as otherwise provided under subsection (c) of this section) as an immigrant under this chapter at the time of examination for adjustment of such alien.

Matter of K-A-, 23 I & N Dec. 661, 666 (BIA 2004) (relief under section 209(b) of the Act is discretionary).

The INA section 209(c) waiver of inadmissibility is not available to aliens who are inadmissible under INA section 212(a)(3)(B) (terrorist activities).

Section 212(a)(3)(B)(i)(I) of the INA, as amended by the REAL ID Act of 2005, describes an alien who is inadmissible and states in pertinent part:

Any alien who . . . (I) has engaged in a terrorist activity. . . is inadmissible.

The INA, at section 212(a)(3)(B)(iv)(VI) defines the term "engaged in terrorist activity," in part, to "commit an act that the actor knows, or reasonably should know, affords material support, including a safe house, transportation, communications, funds, transfer of funds or other material financial benefit, false documentation or identification, weapons (including chemical, biological, or radiological weapons), explosives or training—

Nebraska Service Center

www.uscis.gov

Page 2 of 2

Receipt Number: ████████   Page 2

(aa) for the commission of a terrorist activity;
(bb) to any individual who the actor know, or reasonably should know, has committed or plans to commit a terrorist activity;
(cc) to a terrorist organization described in subclause (I) or (II) of clause (vi), or to any member of such an organization; or
(dd) to a terrorist organization described in clause (vi)(III), or to any member of such an organization, unless the actor can demonstrate by clear and convincing evidence that the actor did not know, and should not have reasonably known, that the organization was a terrorist organization."

The INA, at section 212(a)(3)(B)(vi)(III), defines a terrorist organization as an organization that is a group of two or more individuals, whether organized or not, which engages in, or has a subgroup which engages in, the activities described in subclauses (I) through (VI) of clause (iv).

In your asylum application you provided a statement that you have actively supported the Mujahadin since 1984 when you were twelve years old. You state that you helped carry supplies such as weapons, ammunition, flour, and sugar from Pakistan to Afghanistan to the soldiers fighting there.

According to public information from the Department of State in the April 24, 2002 published "Report for Congress Afghanistan: Challenges and Options for Reconstructing a Stable and Moderate State", the Najibullah (Gilzai Pushtun) government ruled Afghanistan from 1986-1992 Promoted National Reconciliation program in 1986 and promulgated quasi-parliamentary constitution in 1987, strengthened army and tribal militia forces. Najibullah was overthrown by the mujahadin in 1992 and was brutally killed in 1996.

Due to the activities and objectives of the Mujahadin, it meets the current definition of an undesignated terrorist organization at INA section 212(a)(3)(B)(vi)(III). The violent activities of the Mujahadin match those described in section 212(a)(3)(B)(iii) and 212(a)(3)(B)(iv). Because your act(s) of material support of the Mujahadin was voluntary, you are inadmissible under INA section 212(a)(3)(B)(i)(I).

Accordingly, your application must be and hereby is denied. The regulations do not provide for an appeal to this decision.

Sincerely,

F. Gerard Heinauer
Director
NSC/DPM EX246

Nebraska Service Center   www.uscis.gov

D. Description of Waiver Process for Immigration Court Cases

Page 1 of 2

U.S. Citizenship
and Immigration
Services

Fact Sheet   Oct. 23, 2008

**Department of Homeland Security Implements Exemption Authority
for Certain Terrorist-Related Inadmissibility Grounds for Cases with
Administratively Final Orders of Removal**

Under section 212(d)(3)(B)(i) of the Immigration and Nationality Act (INA), the Secretary of Homeland Security may conclude in his sole unreviewable discretion to not apply certain of the terrorist-related grounds of inadmissibility at section 212(a)(3)(B) of the INA. As of Sept. 8, 2008, the Department of Homeland Security (DHS) began implementation of the Secretary's exercise of his exemption authority for certain terrorist-related inadmissibility grounds under section 212(d)(3)(B)(i) of the INA for cases issued administratively final orders of removal by the Department of Justice (DOJ), Executive Office for Immigration Review (EOIR).

The implementation currently covers detained cases with an administratively final order of removal and non-detained cases with an administratively final order of removal that was issued on or after Sept. 8, 2008.

DHS will consider a case for an exemption only after an order of removal is administratively final. An order of removal is generally considered an administratively final order when either a decision by the Board of Immigration Appeals (BIA) affirms an order of removal or the period in which the individual is permitted to seek review of such order by the BIA has expired, whichever date is earlier. By adjudicating the exemption at this stage, all parties will have a chance to litigate the merits of the case up through the BIA, and DHS will be able to focus its resources on cases where the possible exemption is the only issue remaining in the individual's case. The 212(d)(3)(B)(i) exemption will be considered even if the individual files a Petition For Review with a Federal Circuit Court of Appeals.

For individuals who are **not** in U.S. Immigration and Customs Enforcement (ICE) custody (non-detained) and for whom their administratively final order of removal was issued on or after Sept. 8, 2008, the ICE Office of the Chief Counsel handling the case will forward the case to U.S. Citizenship and Immigration Services (USCIS) for exemption consideration if relief or protection was denied **solely** on the basis of one of the grounds of inadmissibility for which exemption authority has been exercised by the Secretary. These individuals and their last attorneys of record will receive in the mail a *Notice of Referral* indicating that their case has been referred to USCIS for consideration of an available exemption to the terrorist-related inadmissibility provisions of the INA. An individual who receives such a notice does not need to take additional steps or contact ICE to initiate the process. However, it is imperative that the individual keep his/her address up to date with USCIS by filing the Form AR-11, *Change of Address*. Also, individuals are reminded that they must continue to comply with ongoing security check requirements. Thus, they may receive notices to update their fingerprints and biometrics during this process at their address on record with USCIS.

Page 2 of 2

If an eligible individual is in ICE custody (detained) upon the issuance of an administratively final order of removal, the ICE Office of the Chief Counsel handling the case will serve the *Notice of Referral* on the individual in coordination with the ICE Office of Detention and Removal Operations (DRO). The individual will also be provided with a Form I-246, *Application for Stay of Deportation or Removal*. The *Notice of Referral* will explain to detained individuals that they must file the attached Form I-246 if they wish to have USCIS consider their eligibility for the 212(d)(3)(B)(i) exemption. In order to be considered for an exemption, the individual who is otherwise eligible for consideration must file the stay of removal request with DRO within seven (7) days of service of the letter. If that individual requests a stay of removal, his or her case will be forwarded to USCIS for consideration of the exemption authority.

USCIS will give priority to certain cases, including those where individuals are detained. The USCIS determination on the exemption is final and within the sole discretion of the Secretary of Homeland Security. Individuals cannot appeal the decision to EOIR. USCIS will directly notify the individual and the appropriate ICE Office of the Chief Counsel of its determination. If USCIS finds that the case merits an exemption, the ICE Office of the Chief Counsel will then forward to the individual a request to join in a *Joint Motion to Reopen* before EOIR. This request will include a template of the *Joint Motion to Reopen*. The individual or, if represented, his/her counsel should sign the motion and return it to the ICE Office of the Chief Counsel. The appropriate Form EOIR-33 (IC or BIA) (Change of Address) with the individual's address information should be forwarded with the motion. If the individual is represented, a Form EOIR-28 (Entry of Appearance – Immigration Court) or Form EOIR-27 (Entry of Appearance – BIA) should be forwarded as well. Upon receipt, ICE will file the *Joint Motion to Reopen* with EOIR, attaching USCIS' grant of the exemption. For *pro se* individuals, if ICE has not received anything from the individual after two weeks, ICE will file an independent Motion to Reopen with a Summary of the Alien's Claim.

Information regarding the implementation of the exemption authority for cases of individuals who are not detained and received an administratively final order of removal before Sept. 8, 2008, will be forthcoming.

8. Endnotes

[1] U.N. Convention Relating to the Status of Refugees, 189 U.N.T.S. 137 (July 28, 1951); U.N. Protocol Relating to the Status of Refugeees, 606 U.N.T.S. 268 (October 4, 1967). The United States played a leading part in the drafting of the 1951 Convention, and bound itself to its substantive provisions in 1968 by acceding to the 1967 Protocol. The United States is also a member of the Executive Committee of the U.N. High Commissioner for Refugees.

[2] Pub.L. No. 96-212, 94 Stat. 102 (1980). As the Supreme Court has confirmed, a primary purpose of Congress in passing the Refugee Act of 1980 "was to bring United States refugee law into conformance with the 1967 United Nations Protocol," which incorporates by reference articles 2 through 34 of the 1951 Convention. *INS v. Cardoza-Fonseca*, 480 U.S. 421, 436 (1987).

[3] INA § 208(b)(2) (8 U.S.C. § 1158(b)(2)) (bars to asylum); INA § 241(b)(3)(B) (8 U.S.C. § 1231(b)(3)(B)) (bars to withholding of removal).

[4] In addition, non-citizens—including those lawfully admitted to the United States or previously granted asylum, refugee status, or other permanent status here—can be deported from the United States for a broad range of violations of law both civil and criminal. The full list of grounds that can make a non-citizen deportable from, or inadmissible to, the United States, and of statutory bars to asylum and withholding of removal, is reproduced in Appendix A of this report.

[5] Human Rights First has had a longstanding interest in the proper application of the "exclusion" clauses of the Refugee Convention, and has conducted research, convened legal experts, and provided guidance to assist in the development of effective and fair methods for excluding those who are rightly barred from refugee protection. It coordinated a special issue of the International Journal of Refugee Law, 12 IJRL Special Supplementary Issue on Exclusion (2000), as part of a multi-year project on exclusion that resulted in the publication of the report *Refugees, Rebels & the Quest for Justice (2002)*. Human Rights First has testified before Congress on these issues and has submitted amicus brief s to U.S. courts on their relevance to asylum and other immigration cases under U.S. law.

[6] "Material support" to an organization engaged in terrorist activity may constitute a "serious non-political crime" justifying exclusion under Article 1F of the Refugee Convention, assuming it is knowing and voluntary, assuming the regularity and value of such contributions are sufficient for the crime to be considered "serious," and assuming that the violence of the group is disproportionate to its political objectives. UNHCR, *Background Note on the Application of the Exclusion Clauses: Article 1F of the 1951 Convention Relating to the Status of Refugees*, September 4, 2003 (available at http://www.unhcr.org/cgi-bin/texis/vtx/refworld/rwmain?docid=3f5857d24&page=search).

[7] Sir Elihu Lauterpacht & Daniel Bethlehem, *The Scope and Content of the Principle of* Non-Refoulement (June 2003) (available at http://www.unhcr.org/cgi-bin/texis/vtx/refworld/rwmain?page=search&docid=470a33af0&skip=0&query=Lauterpacht).

[8] Quoted in Karen De Young, "U.S. to Stop Green Card Denials for Dissidents," *Washington Post*, March 27, 2008.

[9] *Matter of S-K-*, 23 I.&N. Dec. 936, 948 (BIA 2006).

[10] INA § 212(a)(3)(B)(iii)(V); 8 U.S.C. § 1182(a)(3)(B)(iii)(V).

[11] Immigration Act of 1990, Pub. L. No. 101-649, 101 Stat. 4975 (1990).

[12] *Matter of Rodriguez-Majano*, 19 I.&N. Dec. 811 (BIA 1988).

[13] *Matter of Izatula*, 20 I.&N. Dec. 149 (BIA 1990). The BIA's decision indicates that this asylum seeker had been providing the *mujahidin* with food and clothing. It should be noted that had the applicant engaged or assisted in the persecution of others based on their own political opinions, religion, nationality, or ethnicity, he would have been ineligible for asylum under the INA's "persecutor bar," which has been a bar to asylum and withholding of removal in the United States from the time of the passage of the Refugee Act of 1980.

[14] The State Department's report on human rights conditions in Afghanistan for the preceding year (in passages reproduced in the BIA's decision) stated:

> Regime authorities frequently employ torture to punish or to extract information or confessions. The policy is widespread, indicating it has official sanction. Victims often claim that Soviet officials monitor or indirectly control the torture sessions. . . Use of electric shock to sensitive parts of the body, immersion in water, and beatings are common forms of physical abuse reported by victims and witnesses. Threats of abuse against family members and prolonged sleep deprivation are typical forms of psychological abuse. Persistent reports describe cases of mental disturbances induced by torture in regime prisons. . . According to reliable reports, many prisoners died in 1988 as a result of inadequate diet, corporal punishment, and torture. . . [c]itizens have neither the right nor the ability peacefully to change their government.

U.S. Department of State, *1988 Country Reports on Human Rights Practices—Afghanistan* (1989), at 1269, 1273.

[15] See *Matter of S-K-*, 23 I.&N. Dec. 936 (BIA 2006) (discussed in greater detail in Part 4 of this report).

[16] The criminal material support provisions are codified at 18 U.S.C. §§ 2339A and 2339B.

[17] REAL ID Act, Div. B of Pub. L. No. 109-13 § 103, 119 Stat. 231 (2005).

[18] "The 'Material Support' Bar: Denying Refuge to the Persecuted?," *Hearing before the Subcommittee on Human Rights and the Law, Senate Committee on the Judiciary*, 100-Cong., 1· Sess. 23-26 (September 19, 2007) (statement of "Mariana"). Mariana's case has a happy ending. Following her Senate appearance in September 2007, DHS agreed to take jurisdiction over her case back from the immigration court in order to grant her a waiver of the "material support" bar pursuant to a decision by DHS Secretary Chertoff on

September 6, 2007, to make such waivers available to people who were subjected to coercion at the hands of the FARC. She and her daughter were finally granted asylum a few days after her testimony.

[19] In late 2005, for example, an immigration judge granted asylum to a Nepalese medic whom Maoist rebels had forced at gunpoint to treat wounded people. (This man's case is described in greater detail in Part 4 of this report.) Human Rights First provided *pro bono* legal assistance before the immigration courts during the period 2002-2005 to a number of asylum seekers who had been subjected to coercion by armed groups, where neither INS/ICE trial attorneys nor immigration judges took the position that these facts would prohibit a grant of asylum under the immigration law's "terrorism"-related provisions.

[20] The shift in the government's position in the case of a man from Colombia whose asylum claim was litigated during this period was symptomatic of the broader change in the legal policies of the Departments of Justice and Homeland Security. The asylum applicant had managed a farm for an absentee landlord in an area of Colombia that, after he moved there, came under the control of FARC guerrillas. As was their practice in the areas they took over, the guerrillas demanded payment of "taxes" from local landowners. At his employer's instruction, the asylum applicant made payments (of the employer's money) to the armed men who came to the farm to demand and collect it. When the guerrillas later withdrew, paramilitary forces descended on the local inhabitants and targeted those believed to have made payments to the guerrillas. Having narrowly escaped death at the hands of the paramilitaries, the asylum applicant fled to the United States where he applied for protection. The trial attorney who represented DHS before the immigration court in 2003 argued that duress *was* a defense to the "material support" bar but that this man's conduct did not meet the standard for duress. The immigration judge, however, ruled that there were no defenses to the "material support" bar, and the BIA agreed. On appeal to the U.S. Court of Appeals for the Third Circuit, in 2004, Justice Department lawyers representing the government argued that duress was no defense (and, in the alternative, that the applicant would not meet a duress standard). The Third Circuit agreed with the government that the applicant could not meet the high standard for duress, and so did not reach the question of whether such a defense was implicit in the material support bar. *Amaya-Arias v. Ashcroft*, 143 Fed.Appx. 464 (3d Cir. 2005) (unpublished).

[21] *Matter of S-K-*, 23 I.&N. Dec. 936 (BIA 2006); Khan v. Holder, No. 07-72586 (9· Circ. Sept. 9, 2009). While agreeing with the outcome reached by the majority in the Khan case, one of the judges deciding that case noted her concerns about ignoring international law in deciding what conduct should be considered "unlawful," writing:

> The majority recognizes the possibility that an interpretation of "terrorist activity" that ignores international law could lead to some bizarre outcomes, including classifying as terrorists Jews engaged in armed resistance against the Nazis. Maj. Op. at 12774. But such anomalous results are not merely hypothetical: the United States military, whose invasions of Afghanistan and Iraq were indisputably "unlawful" under the domestic laws of those countries, would qualify as a Tier III terrorist organization. Accordingly, any individual or group who assisted the U.S. military in those efforts would be ineligible for asylum or withholding of removal.

Khan at 12785 (Nelson, J., concurring).

[22] It is worth noting that both the Department of Homeland Security and the Department of State, while unwilling to interpret the term "unlawful" in the terrorist activity definition to include unlawfulness under international law binding on the country in question, do not apply the "terrorist activity" definition to the acts of national governments within their national borders, even acts of violence in violation of domestic and international law (many of which would however be targeted by other provisions of the immigration law). The federal agencies appear to deduce this limitation from the term "unlawful," since there is no explicit mention in the "terrorist activity" definition of any limitation of its scope to non-state actors. Similarly, both the Department of Homeland Security and the Department of State are only applying the "terrorist activity" definition to politically motivated violence—a limitation that is likewise not explicitly stated in the immigration law.

[23] Available at http://www.rcusa.org/uploads/pdfs/ms-ltr-jewcomm-7-21-06.pdf.

[24] All of these abuses were corroborated by contemporary human rights reports, including those of the U.S. Department of State. A recent report from Human Rights Watch documents the fact that these abuses continue in Chin State, and that the large numbers of Chin who are forced to flee Burma as a result have been unable to find safety in neighboring India. Human Rights Watch, *"We are Like Forgotten People"–The Chin People of Burma: Unsafe in Burma, Unprotected in India* (January 2009) (available at http://www.hrw.org/en/reports/2009/01/27/we-are-forgotten-people).

[25] Transcripts of hearings before the El Paso Immigration Court, on file with Human Rights First.

[26] The "persecutor bar" to refugee status, asylum, and withholding of removal is codified at sections 101(a)(42), 208(b)(2)(A)(i), and 241(b)(3)(B)(i) of the INA (8 U.S.C. §§ 1101(a)(42), 1158(b)(2)(A)(i), 1231(b)(3)(B)(i)). This provision was—and is—applied to crimes committed by both governmental and non-governmental armed forces, as well as to persecution outside a context of armed conflict.

[27] INA §§ 208(b)(2)(A)(iv) & 241(b)(3)(B)(iv) (8 U.S.C. §§ 1158(b)(2)(A)(iv) & 1231(b)(3)(B)(iv)).

[28] The Immigration Judge wrote:

> [T]he Court finds that the CNF is an individual, or a group of individuals who uses firearms and explosives to endanger the safety of an individual or group of individuals, or to cause substantial property damage. The Court further finds that members of the Burmese military are "individuals" whose safety can be endangered by the use of firearms and/or explosives. The Court further finds that the Burmese military has property that can be substantially damaged by the use of firearms and/or explosives.
>
> The Court specifically finds that Congress made no exception for what most would consider a legitimate armed struggle for freedom against an oppressive military dictatorship. The Court further finds that Congress made no exception for governments whose political legitimacy is questionable.

Immigration Judge decision in *Matter of S-K-* (Feb. 2, 2005) pp. 6-7 (on file with Human Rights First).

[29] 23 I.&N. Dec. 936 (BIA 2006). The BIA issued unpublished decisions along the same lines to all the other Chin applicants whose appeals it considered shortly thereafter.

[30] *Ahmed v. Scharfen*, No. C 08-1680 MHP, 2009 U.S. Dist. LEXIS 591 (N.D. Cal. Jan. 7, 2009).

[31] A recent decision of the U.S. Court of Appeals for the Seventh Circuit noted that the immigration law's description of a "Tier III" group as one that "engages in" what the immigration law defines as "terrorist activity" requires something more than a showing that members of the group have committed acts of violence:

> If an activity is not authorized, ratified, or otherwise approved or condoned by the organization, then the organization is not the actor. NAACP v. Claiborne Hardware Co., 458 U.S. 886, 930-32 (1982). It may be liable under the principles of agency law, even criminally liable, for a harm done by one of its employees or other agents, as when an employee commits a tort within the course of his employment although not authorized to do so by his employer. [Citations omitted] But that

does not mean that the employer "engaged in" the employee's act. An organization is not a terrorist organization just because one of its members commits an act of armed violence without direct or indirect authorization, even if his objective was to advance the organization's goals, though the organization might be held liable to the victim of his violent act.

Hussain v. Mukasey, 518 F.3d 534 (7· Cir. 2008).

[32] The State Department's Foreign Affairs Manual explicitly instructs its officers that the membership bar only applies to present members. 9 *FAM 40.32 n. 5.4* . Both the USCIS Asylum Office and the Refugee & Asylum Law Division have confirmed to Human Rights First that DHS takes the same position with respect to the membership bar, a fact borne out by numerous USCIS decisions denying adjustment of status to persons who indicated that they were members of various alleged "Tier III" groups at the time they applied for asylum and had not indicated to USCIS that their membership had since ceased.

[33] The supplies Jamshid carried as a child were in all likelihood being paid for by the U.S. government, specifically the Central Intelligence Agency (CIA), then under the leadership of current Secretary of Defense Robert Gates.

[34] The White House, Guest List for the First Lady's Box at the 2006 State of the Union (January 31, 2006), available at http://georgewbush-whitehouse.archives.gov/news/releases/2006/01/20060131-12.html

[35] The retroactive application of the "Tier III" definition, to interactions a person had with armed groups before the "Tier III" concept was ever enacted, poses a related set of concerns. The law provides that a person will not be liable for "material support" to a "Tier III" group if he can show by clear and convincing evidence that in making this contribution he did not know, and should not reasonably have known, that the group "was a terrorist organization." It is difficult to give content to this knowledge provision if the "Tier III" definition is applied retroactively to groups that were not defined as "terrorist organizations" at the time even under the immigration laws, and have never been listed or designated as "terrorist organizations" by the U.S. government.

[36] These provisions are described in Part 2 of this report, and are reproduced in Appendix A.

[37] Mimi Hall, "U.S. Has Mandela on Terrorist List," *U.S.A. Today*, April 20, 2008. Seen in comparison with the treatment of refugees and asylum seekers in the United States, the wonder is not that these ANC members were deemed to be inadmissible to the United States, but that they were ever granted waivers. At the time when these ANC leaders were apparently being waived into the United States, there had not been—indeed there still has not been—any general implementation of discretionary authority to waive in people inadmissible based on voluntary associations with "Tier III" groups, whether by the Secretary of State or by the Secretary of Homeland Security. While the Secretary of State was apparently able to grant waivers in these cases without a broader announcement, this has not been done domestically. Had any of these ANC members been applying for permanent residence from the Department of Homeland Security—rather than a temporary visa from the Department of State—their cases would have remained on hold until Congress acted to remove the ANC from the scope of the "Tier III" definition.

[38] Pub. L. No. 110-257, 122 Stat. 2426 (2008).

[39] Statement of Asst. Secretary of State Jendayi Frazer, Opening of the General Interim Headquarters, SPLA (January 29, 2008).

[40] Office to Monitor and Combat Trafficking in Persons, Memorandum of Justification Consistent With the Trafficking Victims Protection Act of 2000, Regarding Determinations With Respect to "Tier 3" Countries, September 14, 2009 (available at: http://www.state.gov/g/tip/rls/other/2009/129593.htm).

[41] Anna Husarska, "Freedom Fighters Need Not Apply," *Washington Post*, December 15, 2008. Copy of denial letter on file with Human Rights First.

[42] Copy of denial letter on file with Human Rights First.

[43] This is particularly odd since northern members of the NDA themselves put military forces in the field beginning in 1997; their involvement in armed conflict was however much briefer and less extensive than that of the SPLA.

[44] One Notice of Intent to Terminate Asylum Status sent in 2009 to an asylee from Ethiopia, for example, stated:

> According to reliable international sources, AAPO [All-Amhara People's Organization] members have conspired and planned violent attacks against the government of Ethiopia. CUD [Coalition for Unity and Democracy], through its association with AAPO and other organizations at a later date meets the current definition of an undesignated terrorist organization. Such activities may indicate inadmissibility grounds according to Sec. 212(a)(3)(B) of the INA (Immigration and Nationality Act).

Copy of letter on file with Human Rights First.

[45] "Iraqi Volunteers, Iraqi Refugees: What Is America's Obligation?" *Hearing Before the Subcommittee on the Middle East and South Asia, House Committee on Foreign Affairs*, 110· Cong., 1· Sess. 31 (March 26, 2007).

[46] DHS, and its predecessor agency the Immigration & Naturalization Service, had long taken the position that duress was no defense to the bar to refugee protection that applies to people who have ordered, incited, assisted, or otherwise participated in the persecution of other people, believing this position to be dictated by the Supreme Court's earlier interpretation of a different statute. The Supreme Court recently held that its earlier precedent did not in fact control the interpretation of the Refugee Act's persecutor bar, so that DHS's application of the persecutor bar to victims of coercion should also be due for re-examination. *Negusie v. Holder*, 555 U.S. ____ (2009).

[47] George Rupp (op-ed), "Terrorist or Terrorized?," *L.A. Times*, March 29, 2006; T. R. Goldman, "Refugees from Oppressive Regimes Kept Out ," *Legal Times*, June 12, 2006.

[48] Copy of asylum application on file with Human Rights First. Quite aside from the other legal objections to such a construction—including the fact that Ziad offered his household goods under duress, and that Persian carpets and antique furniture do not bear much connection to terrorist activity—it was clear from the facts of Ziad's asylum claim that this bribe was not paid to the Taliban as an organization, but to a single corrupt official who was extremely anxious that his colleagues not find out about it.

[49] Numbers provided by USCIS at a September 8, 2009 liaison meeting on the "terrorism-related inadmissibility grounds" of the immigration law.

[50] Memorandum from Jonathan Scharfen, Deputy Director, USCIS, "Processing the Discretionary Exemption to the Inadmissibility Ground for Providing Material Support to Certain Terrorist Organizations" (May 24, 2007), available at http://www.uscis.gov/files/pressrelease/MaterialSupport_24May07.pdf.

[51] Application for asylum and correspondence with USCIS on file with Human Rights First.

[52] All U.S. jurisdictions recognize that youth is a substantial mitigating factor with respect to criminal activity, and may constitute a complete defense to criminal liability. *See, e.g., Roper v. Simmons*, 543 U.S. 551 (2005). International law has also long recognized the special vulnerabilities of children and afforded them special protections in situations of armed conflict. In 1999, the United States was one of the first countries to ratify the International Labor Organization Convention on the Prohibition and Immediate Action for the Elimination of the Worst Forms of Child Labor, which recognizes the forced recruitment of children under the age of 18 for use in armed conflict as one of the worst forms of child labor. I.L.O. 182, June 17, 1999, 38 I.L.M. 1207. In 2002, the United States ratified the Optional Protocol to the Convention on the Rights of the Child on the Involvement of Children in Armed Conflict, which set 18 as the minimum age for direct participation in hostilities, prohibited the conscription of persons under the age of 18 by government forces, and barred non-state armed groups from recruiting or using in hostilities children under the age of 18 under any circumstances. CA Res./54/.263, U.N. Doc. A/RES/54/9, Annex I (May 25, 2000).

[53] Copy of denial letter on file with Human Rights First.

[54] *Singh-Kaur v. Ashcroft*, 385 F.3d 292 (3d Cir. 2004).

[55] *See, e.g., Matter of S-K-*, 23 I.&N. 936, 945 (BIA 2006) (noting—but not deciding on—DHS's argument that the "material support" bar "was intended to cover "virtually all forms of assistance, even small monetary contributions").

[56] Copies of asylum application and immigration court and BIA briefing on file with Human Rights First. Human Rights First filed an *amicus* brief to the BIA in support of Louis' appeal.

[57] Copy of application for asylum and motion to reopen application for adjustment of status on file with Human Rights First. Solomon had in fact not been a member of the OLF for several years by the time his application for permanent residence was denied, but because neither he nor his attorneys had any reason to think such membership would pose a problem for his application, he had had no reason to specify this fact to USCIS at the time of filing.

[58] INA § 212(a)(3)(B)(iiii), (iv) (8 U.S.C. § 1182(a)(3)(B)(iii), (iv)). (The full text of these provisions is reproduced in Appendix A.)

[59] Immigration Judge decision dated February 2, 2009, on file with Human Rights First.

[60] ABSDF members were involved, for example, in distributing within Burma publications such as the *New Era Journal*, a monthly newspaper published by Burmese exiles on the Thai-Burma border that attempted to stimulate democratic debate among its readers and contributors, and received much of its funding from the Open Society Institute. http://www.unhcr.org/refworld/country,,,QUERYRESPONSE,MMR,,3df4be1634,0.html

[61] Copy of denial letter on file with Human Rights First.

[62] Copy of denial letter on file with Human Rights First. The basis for DHS's characterization of NAMIR (a constitutional-monarchist group that dwindled after its leader, Shahpour Bakhtiar, was assassinated in exile in Paris by agents of the Khomeini regime in 1991) as a "Tier III terrorist organization" is unclear from this denial letter, which cites to a reference in a 1991 publication to "claims that the group 'resorted to violence in Iran in 1984 with a series of car bombings in Tehran and a rocket attack on a regional militia headquarters at Rezaiyeh'" and to another document—for which the denial letter provides a non-functioning internet address—that apparently stated that the group "staged an unsuccessful coup against the Ayatollah Khomeini regime." Human Rights First has been unable to identify the sources of these claims or to substantiate them through searches of other publicly available sources. A 1987 country study published by the Federal Research Division of the Library of Congress, for example, states that "[w]ith the notable exception of the Mojahedin and the ethnic Kurdish parties, the expatriate opposition parties [among which NAMIR is named] eschewed the use of political violence to achieve their shared goal of overthrowing the regime in Tehran." See Helen Chapman Metz, ed., *Iran, A Country Study*, GPO for the Library of Congress (1987), available at http://countrystudies.us/iran/96.htm .

[63] Copy of denial letter on file with Human Rights First.

[64] Library of Congress catalog listing for the *Oromo Commentary* is available at http://catalog.loc.gov/cgi-bin/Pwebrecon.cgi?DB=local&Search_Arg=Oromo+Commentary&Search_Code=TKEY%5E*&CNT=100&hist=1&type=quick. Some of the early issues of *The Kindling Point* are available at the website www.gumii.org.

[65] This essay is quoted extensively in Eloi Ficquet, *De la chair imbibée de foi: la viande comme marqueur de la frontière entre chrétiens et musulmans en Ethiopie*, Anthropology of Food (May 2006) (available at http://aof.revues.org/index105.html).

[66] Information provided by Fatmushe's attorney.

[67] Human Rights First interview with Aashaa, October 5, 2009. Copy of asylum application on file with Human Rights First.

[68] "The 'Material Support' Bar: Denying Refuge to the Persecuted?," *Hearing before the Subcommittee on Human Rights and the Law, Senate Committee on the Judiciary*, 100· Cong., 1· Sess. 138 (September 19, 2007) (statement of Physicians for Human Rights).

[69] The principle that physicians must treat a patient's health as their highest priority goes back to the Hippocratic Oath, and is at the core of later expressions of medical ethics. The International Code of Medical Ethics, for example, affirms that "A physician shall always act in the patient's best interest when providing medical care. . . A physician shall give emergency care as a humanitarian duty unless he/she is assured that others are willing and able to give such care." World Medical Association, International Code of Medical Ethics, adopted by the 3d Assembly of the World Medical Assocation, London, 1949 (as amended). The Declaration of Geneva (a modern physican's oath and statement of ethical principles, also adopted by the World Medical Association) also emphasizes the obligation to treat patients without discrimination based on race, religion, political affiliation, or other factors. Both documents are available at http://www.wma.net/en/30publications/10policies/c8/index.html.

[70] Copies of immigration court and BIA filings and decisions on file with Human Rights First.

[71] Physicians for Human Rights filed an amicus brief to the Board of Immigration Appeals in B.T.'s case that provides an overview of relevant principles of medical ethics and international law. A copy of that brief is available at http://physiciansforhumanrights.org/library/documents/testimony/amicus-brief-material-support.pdf.

[72] The U.S. Army Field Manual, for example, requires that the wounded and sick in enemy hands "shall be treated humanely and cared for by the Party to the conflict in whose power they may be, without any adverse distinction founded on sex, race, nationality, religion, political opinions, or any other similar criteria," and "shall not willfully be left without medical assistance and care." U.S. Army Field Manual No. 27-10, "The Law of Land Warfare," § 215, Department of the Army, 1956. Other branches of the U.S. Armed Services have provided similar guidance, with the Navy, for example, instructing that "wounded and sick personnel falling into enemy hands must be . . . cared for without adverse distinction." The United States Commander's Handbook on the Law of Naval Operations, NWP 1-14, "The Law of Naval Warfare," §11-4, Department of the Navy, 1995.

[73] Department of Defense, Instruction, Subject: Medical Program Support for Detainee Operations, 2310.08E, 4.1.1 & 4.1.2 (June 6, 2006).

[74] U.S. Department of State, *Country Reports on Human Rights Practices 1999—Serbia-Montenegro* (Feb. 23, 2000); *Country Reports on Human Rights Practices 1999—*Russia (Feb. 23, 2000); *Country Reports on Human Rights Practices—Colombia* 2002 (Mar. 31, 2003).

[75] INA § 212(a)(3)(B)(i)(IX) (8 U.S.C. § 1182(a)(3)(B)(i)(IX).

[76] Copies of application for asylum and of letters denying permanent residence on file with Human Rights First.

[77] Copy of denial letter on file with Human Rights First. The mother's application for permanent residence was still pending at the time her young son's application was denied.

[78] Copies of multiple denial letters on file with Human Rights First.

[79] Correspondence and conversation with applicant's attorney; copy of denial letter on file with Human Rights First.

[80] Correspondence and conversation with applicant's attorney; copy of denial letter on file with Human Rights First.

[81] Available at http://www.rcusa.org/ms-sgnltr-faithorgbush8-24-06.pdf.

[82] USA PATRIOT Act, 115 Stat. 272 (2001) at § 411(a)(1)(F)(VI) (amending INA § 212(a)(3)(B)(iv) (8 U.S.C. § 1182(a)(3)(B)(iv)).

[83] Refugee Council U.S.A., *U.S. Refugee Admissions Program for Fiscal Year 2006 and 2007: The Impact of the Material Support Bar—Recommendations of Refugee Council USA* (available at http://www.rcusa.org/uploads/pdfs/RCUSA2006finpostbl-w.pdf).

[84] *Matter of S-K-*, 23 I.&N. Dec. 936, 942, n. 7 (BIA 2006).

[85] Representatives of DHS and the Department of Justice emphasized the discretionary, unreviewable nature of the waiver in public discussions and testimony before Congress. *See, e.g.,* "Current Issues in U.S. Refugee Protection and Resettlement," *Hearing Before the Subcommittee on Africa, Global Human Rights and International Operations, House Committee on International Relations,* 109· Cong., 2d Sess. 34 (May 10, 2006) (statement of Rachel Brand, Office of Legal Policy, DOJ).

[86] U.S. Commission on International Religious Freedom, 2006 Annual Report, May 1, 2006, at 69 (available at http://www.uscirf.gov/images/AR2006/2006annualrpt.pdf). The USCIRF is a bipartisan independent government commission, established pursuant to the International Religious Freedom Act of 1998 to monitor violations of the right to freedom of thought, conscience, and religion or belief abroad, and to give independent policy recommendations to the President, Secretary of State, and Congress.

[87] Exercises of Authority Under Sec. 212(d)(3)(B)(i) of the Immigration & Nationality Act, May 3, 2006 (State Department waiver for Burmese Karen refugees in Tham Hin Camp, Thailand); August 24, 2006 (State Department waiver for Karen refugees in additional camps in Thailand); January 22, 2007 (State Department waiver applicable to persons having provided material support to the KNU/KNLA regardless of their ethnicity or location); Exercise of Authority under Sec. 212(d)(3)(B)(i) of the Immigration & Nationality Act, March 6, 2007 (DHS waiver announcement for persons having provided material support to the KNU/KNLA and seven other groups).

[88] *See, e.g.,* Editorial, "U.S. Denies Refuge to Friends, the Abused," *Minneapolis-St. Paul Star Tribune,* January 9, 2007; Darryl Fears, "Conservatives Decry Terror Laws' Impact on Refugees," *Washington Post,* January 8, 2007.

[89] Left out of these initial waiver announcements were supporters of Hmong and Montagnard ethnic minority members who had been allied with U.S. forces during the Vietnam War. Their omission was due to definitional difficulties on the part of the federal agencies involved, who were initially stymied by the fact that "the Hmong" and "the Montagnards" were not in fact "terrorist organizations" but rather ethnic groups. In addition, a number of the cases of Hmong and Montagnard refugees being affected by the "terrorism bars" involved people who had actually fought, rather than providing support to those who did, and the statutory waiver authority as it stood at the time did not cover former combatants. DHS and the State Department finally issued waivers of the "material support" bar for persons associated with Hmong and Montagnard combatants in October 2007.

[90] Even once congressional amendments were enacted as part of the Consolidated Appropriations Act that removed the Chin National Front from the immigration law's definition of a "terrorist organization," this man's release from custody was delayed due to DHS and DOJ's failure effectively to disseminate this information, and its implications, to immigration judges and DHS trial attorneys in local areas.

[91] "The 'Material Support' Bar: Denying Refuge to the Persecuted?," *Hearing before the Subcommittee on Human Rights and the Law, Senate Committee on the Judiciary,* 100· Cong., 1· Sess. 8-12 (September 19, 2007).

[92] Id.

[93] Consolidated Appropriations Act, 2008, Pub. L. 110-161, 121 Stat. 1844., Div. J, § 691.

[94] Information provided by applicant's attorney.

[95] U.S. Department of State, Background Note: Bangladesh (May 2009), available at http://www.state.gov/r/pa/ei/bgn/3452.htm .

[96] Marisa Taylor, "U.S. allies losing asylum bids over definition of 'terrorist,'" *McClatchy Newspapers,* May 2, 2009.

[97] Karen DeYoung, Stalwart Service for U.S. in Iraq Is Not Enough to Gain Green Card, *Washington Post*, March 23,2008; Karen DeYoung, U.S. To Stop Green Card Denials for Dissidents, *Washington Post*, March 27, 2008.

[98] USCIS TRIG ("Terrorism-related Inadmissibility Ground") Liaison Meeting, September 8. 2009.

[99] Memorandum from Jonathan Scharfen, Deputy Director, USCIS, "Withholding Adjudication and Review of Prior Denials of Certain Categories of Cases Involving Association With, or Provision of Material Support to, Certain Terrorist Organizations or Other Groups" (Mar. 26, 2008), available at http://www.uscis.gov/files/nativedocuments/Withholding_26Mar08.pdf

[100] Anna Husarska, "Freedom Fighters Need Not Apply," *Washington Post*, December 15, 2008.

[101] That waiver decision by DHS and the State Department was made by Secretaries Clinton and Napolitano on September 21, 2009, and announced publicly a month later. A copy of the announcement is available at http://www.uscis.gov/portal/site/uscis/menuitem.5af9bb95919f35e66f614176543f6d1a/?vgnextoid=f3d233e559274210VgnVCM100000082ca60aRCRD&vgnextchannel=f 39d3e4d77d73210VgnVCM100000082ca60aRCRD .

[102] While doctors and others who provided medical care under duress are being considered for waivers, USCIS is maintaining on hold other pending cases that involve medical professionals who treated patients "voluntarily," that is, as a matter of professional duty rather than coercion. USCIS TRIG Liaison Meeting, September 8, 2009.

[103] As described by the State Department, listing or designating a group as a terrorist organization "supports our efforts to curb terrorism financing and to encourage other nations to do the same; stigmatizes and isolates designated terrorist organizations internationally; deters donations or contributions to or economic transactions with a named organization; heightens public awareness and knowledge of terrorist organizations; [and] signals to other governments our concern about named organizations." Office of the Coordinator for Counterterrorism, U.S. Dep't of State, "Foreign Terrorist Organizations" (July 7, 2009), available at http://www.state.gov/s/ct/rls/other/des/123085.htm.

[104] A country study published by the Federal Research Division of the Library of Congress in 1988 provides the following account of FLAM activities in the mid-1980's:

> FLAM members have claimed responsibility for distributing a highly articulate, fifty-page pamphlet entitled "Le Manifeste du Négro-Mauritanien Opprimé" (The Manifesto of the Oppressed Black Mauritanian), documenting alleged examples of officially sanctioned discrimination. Copies of the manifesto were circulated in Addis Ababa during the spring 1986 summit meetins of the OAU and during the summer 1986 summit meetings of the Nonaligned Movement in Harare, Zimbabwe. FLAM adherents were also charged with instigating a series of attacks in September and October 1986 against a fish-processing facility in Nouadhibou, a pharmacy and gas station in Nouakchott, and three government vehicles. Although damage from the attacks was minimal, they were the first such acts of sabotage in Mauritania and thus represented a dramatic escalation in political violence.

Robert E. Handloff, ed., *Mauritania, A Country Study*, GPO for the Library of Congress (1988) (available at http://lcweb2.loc.gov/frd/cs/mrtoc.html#mr0107).

[105] See, e.g., Anthony G. Pazzanita, *Historical Dictionary of Mauritania* (3· Ed. 2008), at 200-202.

[106] In response to Mohamed's petition for a writ of *mandamus* from the federal district court to order the Department of Homeland Security to process his application for permanent residence, the Chief of Staff of the USCIS Nebraska Service Center filed a declaration stating that FLAM "has carried out sporadic armed attacks against government targets since its creation in 1983." The affidavit cites no sources for this statement and provides no further information on the timing of FLAM's armed activities. Declaration of Neil M. Jacobson, Chief of Staff, USCIS Nebraska Service Center, April 27, 2009 (copy on file with Human Rights First).

[107] DHS's February 2008 denial of permanent residence to an asylee from Ethiopia, for example, explained why DHS believed him to be "a member of a terrorist organization:"

> The Terrorism Knowledge Base (TKB), developed by the Memorial Institute for the Prevention of Terrorism (MIPT), offers in-depth information on terrorist incidents, groups and trials. According to public information on this site, the EPRA [Ethiopian People's Revolutionary Army] "was formed in 1976 and was primarily active in the Tigray and Gondar regions, where it fought both the Ethiopian military and other opposition groups, primarily the Tigray People's Liberation Front (TPLF)." The TKB claims that the EPRA was responsible for 3 incidents between 1986 and 1988.

The letter provides no information about the "incidents" in question. As the denial letter itself states, this asylee joined the Ethiopian People's Revolutionary Party (EPRP) in 2002. Copy of denial letter on file with Human Rights First.

[108] Information provided by Dorjee's attorney.

[109] Memorandum from Michael Aytes, Acting Deputy Director, USCIS, *Implementation of Section 691 of Division J of the Consolidated Appropriations Act, 2008, and Updating Processing Requirements for Discretionary Exemptions to Terrorist Activity Inadmissibility Grounds* (July 28, 2008), at 5.

[110] USCIS TRIG Liaison Meeting, September 8, 2009.

[111] Copy of Notice of Intent to Terminate on file with Human Rights First.

[112] Copy of Notice of Intent to Terminate issued to asylee from Ethiopia, on file with Human Rights First.

[113] Hearing Before the Subcommittee on Human Rights and the Law, Senate Committee on the Judiciary, "Casualties of War: Child Soldiers and the Law," 110· Cong., 1· Sess. 73 (April 24, 2007 (statement of Sen. Richard Durbin).

[114] Child Soldier Accountability Act, Pub. L. No. 110-340, 122 Stat. 3735 (2008).

[115] Child Soldier Prevention Act of 2008, Pub. L. No. 110-457, 122 Stat. 5089 (2008).

[116] Hearings before the Subcommittee on Human Rights and the Law, Senate Committee on the Judiciary, "Casualties of War: Child Soldiers and the Law," 110· Cong., 1· Sess., April 24, 2007, and "The 'Material Support' Bar: Denying Refuge to the Persecuted?" 110· Cong., 1· Sess., September 19, 2007.

[117] Another example profiled in this report is that of Jamshid, the asylee from Afghanistan whose situation is described in Part 4.

[118] S TRIG Liaison Meeting, September 8, 2009.

[119] Id.

[120] Asylum is a better form of relief for a person who is found to be a refugee, as it provides more secure status in the United States, facilitates integration into the U.S. community, and allows for family reunification, which protection under the Convention Against Torture does not. Because of this, most immigration judges who are granting asylum never reach the issue of an asylum applicant's alternative eligibility for protection under the Convention Against Torture.

[121] It is unclear why the mere filing of a motion for reconsideration of the BIA order by ICE should prevent USCIS from considering the case for a waiver. Filing a motion for reconsideration or reopening before the BIA does not affect the finality of a BIA order unless the BIA orders reconsideration or reopening or grants a stay of its original order. ICE here did not request a stay of the BIA's order. This is particularly frustrating in this particular case, where the only basis for the motion for reconsideration was a claimed ambiguity in its text, on a point irrelevant to USCIS's waiver consideration, and on which Kumar's attorney has already indicated that he agrees with (and is prepared to stipulate to) the government's understanding of what the BIA's original decision held.

[122] In two recent cases represented *pro bono* through Human Rights First's legal representation program, for example, where asylum applicants won appeals to the Board of Immigration Appeals and were then sent back down to the immigration court solely for the purpose of confirming that security and background checks were current and for the immigration court to enter an order granting asylum, that purely bureaucratic remand process took nine months in one case and five and a half months in the other. None of those delays were attributable to the applicants. These cases did not involve any "terrorism"-related issues.

[123] USCIS TRIG ("Terrorism-related Inadmissibility Ground") Liaison Meeting, December 11, 2008.

[124] Copies of ICE motion and of applicant's supplemental memorandum of law and opposition to ICE motion to recalendar on file with Human Rights First.

[125] Copies of BIA decision and of asylum seeker's appellate brief on file with Human Rights First.

[126] *Matter of S-K-*, 23 I.&N. Dec. 936, 942, n. 7 (BIA 2006).

[127] Quoted in T.R. Goldman, "Refugees from Oppressive Regimes Kept Out," *Legal Times*, June 12, 2006.

[128] For more information on the detention of asylum seekers in the United States, see Human Rights First, U.S. Detention of Asylum Seekers: Seeking Protection, Finding Prison (April 2009–revised June 2009) (available at http://www.humanrightsfirst.org/pdf/090429-RP-hrf-asylum-detention-report.pdf).

[129] Copies of immigration court submissions on file with Human Rights First.

[130] See Appendix D.

[131] Copy of immigration filings on file with Human Rights First.

[132] Copies of immigration court and BIA decisions on file with Human Rights First.

[133] USCIS TRIG Liaison Meeting, September 8. 2009.

[134] Information provided by asylee's attorney; copies of correspondence from USCIS confirming that asylee relative petitions are on hold on "terrorism"-related grounds on file with Human Rights First.

[135] Human Rights First correspondence and interview with Tashi, October 5, 2009. Copies of application for asylum and of subsequent correspondence with USCIS on file with Human Rights First.

[136] Copy of correspondence on file with Human Rights First. Other information provided to Human Rights First by Photoson.